Look for Normal

Karen Harmon

Edited by Sharon Bodner

Tellwell Talent
www.tellwell.ca

ISBN
978-0-2288-0253-2 (Hardcover)
978-0-2288-0252-5 (Paperback)

ACKNOWLEDGEMENTS

My memories that I hold dear to my heart
are dedicated to my parents.
I am thankful for their life long gift of empathy and humour.

**

Paul – Thank you for always believing in me, for
reminding me that I am smart, for telling me that I am
beautiful, and for laughing at my dumb jokes. Xo
Jessica – Thank you for giving me sincere heart-bursting joy.
Emma – Thank you for teaching us all how to
have a completely open, loving heart.
Mackenzie – Thank you for never letting success get to
our heads, and never letting failure get to our hearts.
Linda – Thank you for being an example of giving
and connecting with those who need a friend.
Doug – Thank you for showing us how
brains and humour work together.
Ken – Thank you for appreciating and loving all that is good.

Bike Trip Friends – Thanks for the lessons in taking turns,
playing nice, inviting adventure, and always propelling forward.
Homies – Thanks for keeping me in prayer
and believing there is a loving God.
Mary – Thanks for being my BFF until death
do us part and longer if necessary.
Barb – Thanks for demonstrating how
faith and family come first.
Fitness Participants – Fitness is forever and
you all give back more than I give you.

**

Special thanks to my favourite writers, **Colleen Friesen** and **Mary Edigar**, who inspired me and influenced me as a writer, and who both gave me motivation and courage when inadequacy crept in. This book would not be possible without the help of **Sophia Jones.** Her brilliance at sentence structure and grammar never cease to amaze me. Thank you. **Sharon Bodner** – A true gift from God, who took me under her wing and cleaned up my whole project with her editing knowledge and wisdom. Thank you.

Please read this book knowing that it is meant as a tribute to my parents, a keepsake for my children, and a salutation to the City of Vancouver and North Vancouver From 1930-1972 and so on.....

Looking for Normal

CHAPTER 1

Leaving Normal

"Normal is just a setting on your dryer"
Erma Bombeck 1927-1996

FRANCES HATED HER MOTHER. SHE WAS TAUGHT BY THE NUNS that it was not "Biblical" to hate. So, she decided to leave her mother and the Catholic Church all in one fell swoop. Both forces in her life had deceived and criticised her. In Frances's eyes, both were hypocritical.

As she waited to board the train for Vancouver, British Columbia in the spring of 1941, Frances took one last look at her family. Standing on the platform with them, she felt adventurous and defiant, with no fear of the unknown as she bravely embarked on this journey towards her future.

Going over in her mind the blur of the last nineteen years that had led her to this decision to leave, brought instant realization of what she was actually doing. She was physically and mentally abandoning this town, her family, and all the narrow-minded, crazy people in it. Frances asked herself how the hell she got to this point in the first place.

Her mother had victimised her for the last time. This was the last straw, Mother, the icing on the cake, with a cherry on top, she thought disdainfully.

FRANCES'S MOTHER, EDITH GERVAIS, ALL FIVE FEET TWO INCHES of her, was dressed flawlessly from head to toe. Floral dress, fur jacket, buckle up shoes, tapestry purse, velvet gloves, and matching hat with veil. Her brightly coloured pink cheeks were delicately brushed over creamy white pancake foundation. One could never miss her crimson red lipstick, shadowed eyes, and the tightest of girdles, possibly why her eyes popped as they did, resembling a deer caught in headlights. Those eyes now held a vacant and disinterested look instead of their usual demure expression, A.K.A. Bette Davis. Edith Gervais, the station agent's wife.

Borderline personality disorder (BPD) is a serious mental illness that centres on the inability to manage emotions effectively. The disorder occurs in the context of relationships; sometimes all relationships are affected, sometimes only one. It usually begins during adolescence or early adulthood.

Most people who suffer from borderline personality disorder have problems regulating their emotions and thoughts, impulsive and reckless behaviour, and unstable relationships, often saying and doing hurtful things that they do not mean, or more times than not, will regret later.

Other disorders, such as depression, anxiety, eating disorders, substance abuse and other personality disorders can often exist along with BPD.

Officially recognized in 1980 by the psychiatric community, BPD has historically met with widespread misunderstanding and blatant stigma. [1]

In her lifetime Edith would never be diagnosed or treated with Borderline Personality Disorder. She would only be considered difficult, strange, a little off, hard to handle, or ultimately, (the most commonly used description of Frances's mother and her sister Violet) just plain crazy.

Frances's father, Joseph Gervais, the station agent of the small rural town that Frances had called home, stood next to her mother. Joseph Gervais was a friend to drifters, floaters, and hoboes. Gentle, kind, and smart as a whip, he was born in the French quarter of Montreal. As a young businessman he had made his way west to Alberta, the province of opportunity. Joe was a successful man, clothed in a three-piece suit by 5:00 a.m. each morning, ready to start his day, even though his job as station agent was unquestionably twenty four hours a day. Needing to be alert and on stand-by for telegraphs and the midnight run through Taber, heading for Lethbridge, Joe Gervais had a lot of responsibility.

There were many vagrant down and outers, riding the rails often looking for handouts. It was not odd at all for one to come calling at any hour of the day or night. Joe offered room and board, a warm bed, and hot soup in exchange for odd jobs around the station, which was also the family home.

Frances assessed her father now with his hat perched atop his balding head, still so handsome. How hard he had worked all these years, managing the station in addition to looking after her mother. Joseph and Edith were side by side but not touching, waiting quietly, patiently on the platform in Taber, for the train that would snatch their daughter up at any moment. Train #401 would soon be whisking Frances off for the adventure of a lifetime.

Thoughts of her mother now frayed at Frances's nerves like nails down the chalkboard. How had Edith managed to conceal her indiscretions, sordid affairs, and blatant narcissism? Was Frances the only one who could see it? Her father had also worked to cover up her sister Violet's angry outbursts, screaming and yelling matches, and self-seeking dalliances. Joe had his hands full.

Violet, six years older than Frances, was much later to be diagnosed as having a personality disorder, and maybe even schizophrenia, a term and diagnosis that none of them would be familiar with until many years down the line. It was too late for help, too late for a relationship, and Frances pitied them all. Poor father. Poor me, she thought.

Surprisingly enough, Violet was there to see her off, though impatiently tapping her toe and craning her neck, trying to see around the bend in the track, anxiously awaiting the train. She was no doubt thinking that it should be her, not Frances, who was getting the opportunity to leave. Out of character, Violet had brought flowers, nervously twisting and turning the stems around her gloved fingers.

It was at this point that Frances noticed her sister's beauty. Without exception Violet would always be referred to as the pretty one, with black hair, dark, deep-set eyes, and alabaster-clear complexion. Violet, pretty. Frances, plain. It was just a known fact, one that Frances no longer cared about. Her sister could be charming when she wanted something, kind when it benefitted her, shrewd and manipulative, especially with their mother. In their mother's eyes, Violet could do no wrong, even when caught smoking and drinking beer behind the school with George Funk the town drunk, twice her age.

GEORGE CALLED HIMSELF A RELIGIOUS MAN—HYPOCRISY THROUGH and through to the core of his very being! Frances burned with anger at the very thought of old drunk George, abandoning his wife and four children, picking up Violet in his old Ford pickup truck to go who knows where. Then, come Sunday, George would appear polished and clear faced at church for confession. Violet would be there as well, sitting alongside her doting mother, suspicious father, and irritated sister.

In Catholic teaching, the Sacrament of Penance is the method by which the congregation confesses sins committed in their day to day life; sins that have been absolved by God (no matter how often they occur) through the administration of a Priest.

"Say, 'Bless me Father, for I have sinned. It's been X days, months, or years since my last confession.' Tell the priest about the hurtful actions you thought of earlier. Rather than giving him a long list of sins, take the opportunity to be open and honest with the confession."

Violet was beautiful, and undeniably insane. Since she was a toddler Violet was given Coca-Cola in her baby bottle because it was recommended for soothing the active child.

Coca-Cola was developed in 1886 by an Atlanta pharmacist, Doctor John S. Pemberton. He created the distinctive beverage to be purchased at soda fountains and it was believed to relieve anxiety in all ages. Originally intended as a patent medicine, until 1903 Coca-Cola contained a significant dose of cocaine. Pemberton chose to mix his coca-leaf extract with sugar syrup, also adding kola-nut extract, giving Coca-Cola the second half of its name, as well as an extra jolt of caffeine.

While cocaine-infused beverages may seem far-fetched now, these drinks were quite common in the late 19th century. Cocaine was not made illegal in the United States until 1914. Cocaine tonics and pills were believed to cure a variety of illnesses, from impotence to asthma, nausea, constipation, fatigue, and headaches.

Over time cocaine became widely used and abused, leading the Coca-Cola Company's then manager, Asa Griggs Candler, to remove all cocaine from the company's beverages. Coke would not become completely cocaine-free until 1929, when scientists perfected the process of removing all psychoactive elements from the coca-leaf extract. According to the New York Times, the Coca-Cola Company was continuing to import coca leaves from Peru and Bolivia until at least the late 1980's. One of the most famous advertising slogans in Coca-Cola history "The Pause That Refreshes" first appeared in the Saturday Evening Post in 1929 and is still used in marketing to this day. [2]

Frances, the plain one, was leaving them. Always self-conscious of her thin, straight blonde hair and clear pale blue eyes, continuously insecure about her height, 5 feet 10 inches, she now towered over her family on this last day. She glanced down to her feet and then shuddered at the monstrosity of them, always knowing they were exceptionally big. "She will never be petite," she could still hear her mother whispering to the store clerks. Later, Edith opted to order through the Eaton's catalogue, relishing in the excitement of its quarterly arrival, even though they did not carry shoes big enough for Frances. She remembered the painful scrunching of her toes into shoes two sizes too small. Frances could often be seen hobbling around town in a slouching and ungainly manner. "Stand up straight," her mother would scold. "Why can't you be more like your sister Violet?" The hurtful words were now running in circles in Frances's head, tormenting her unceasingly. Frances would find solace in her books, her beloved novels, where she could stay forever entranced in another world of literature. She could often be found, shoulders curved, long hair covering her eyes, walking through town with her nose in a book. "There goes Billy the bookworm," she would overhear as she passed by. Frances loved her nick name and was not offended in the least.

SNAPPING BACK TO THE PRESENT TIME, FRANCES STOOD UP A little taller and remembered her dream of becoming a writer or a private investigator, knowing in her heart that the options were endless. If there's a will, there's a way, Frances always chanted to herself whenever she was told that she could not do something. At this time all that mattered, here and now, was holding the train ticket in her clenched hand. Somehow, everything would be all right. The waiting was the only hard part, she realized.

As they waited, the four of them marking time, Frances stared at her mother's face, unable to make any sense of her. Her eyes filled with tears, but she willed them not to fall. The wind began to pick up as it so often did in this prairie town. Frances pulled her collar a little tighter around her neck, wondering what it would be like to have a mother's arm around her; a knowing glance, a warm cuddle, a few words of wisdom to send her on her way. Instead she felt nothing except her mother's coldness, knew nothing but her mother's lies for as far back as she could remember.

THE TERM "DEPRESSION" WOULD COME BACK TO HAUNT FRANCES years from now. Bi-Polar Disorder would raise its unwanted head later in her lifetime. Doctors, psychologists, therapists, or even research for its genetic long-term effects were far from anyone's mind on this day. For all anyone could figure in the 1930s, when someone acted strangely or overly dramatic, it was "crazy behaviour" or "wicked." Sometimes women were even described as witches or bitches.

All Frances could think about was the past nineteen years of trying to withstand her mother's and sister's bizarre, often mean behaviour. Since the day that Frances entered the world and the day that she was bundled up to go home, she had been surrounded by mental illness. It appeared her sister and mother had something wrong, something flawed within them, and were not like other people. There was the silent treatment that Frances and her father experienced; the bouts of endless spending; the numerous times of refurnishing the station house. Often Frances would return from school to see an entirely different living room. Out with the old and in with the new, Edith always announced. Frances was also frequently left to sit over a cold supper at the dinner table, forced to stay until her plate was clean but stubbornly refusing to do so, which meant missing time outside with friends, and only being excused to go to bed.

Finally coming to the conclusion that something had been amiss all these years, is what saved her. The common sense, gentleness, and normalcy of her father was her saving grace. He was her confidante and best friend, her rock, seeing her through and bringing her to this final goodbye.

FRANCES HAD BEEN BORN IN PURPLE SPRINGS, A SMALL HAMLET east of Taber. When Frances left the hospital after her birth on February 26, 1922, her mother did not join her. She was not carried out in loving arms as one would expect. Her mother stayed in the sickly green hospital room, staying behind for three more months with severe depression, unable to cope, or so the story went. Tiny, innocent Frances was left on her own to cry herself to sleep. Scheduled feeding times consisted of being propped up with a baby bottle filled with canned milk—Carnation Evaporated Milk. It was all the rage then. Breastfeeding ruined a ladies' figure, while nurturing and cuddling a baby would spoil the child. In all truth, Frances believed that canned milk turned her onto sugar and fat at the grand old age of one day old. Thanks for nothing!

Coming back to the present, Frances became aware of her friend Ruth standing beside her on the platform. It would be tricky saying goodbye to Ruth, her best friend and confidante, and favourite person of all time. Frances wondered if she would ever have another friend like Ruth. Ruth had always been painfully shy. This saddened Frances, but it had also made her extroverted whenever they were together. Ruth gave Frances courage, as Ruth was also considered plain, but much sweeter and smaller in stature. What a sight they were together, a real Mutt and Jeff pair. Joe always referred to them as the "gold dust twins", a kind and endearing term of the day.

Frances treasured Ruth's infectious giggle. She often exclaimed through fits of laughter, "Oh Billy, you mustn't," whenever Frances teased her about Gordon Nugent having eyes for her. Ruth's undying friendship towards her would be etched in her heart for all of eternity as she left behind her town—their town—and all of the childhood memories it contained. This town had watched her grow, and carried her through her adolescent, awkward years. Yet she had watched this town closer than it had watched her.

Taber, Alberta, the once oasis that grew murky with age, but was still transparent. Frances decided right then and there that she would not miss the flat and rolling prairie, the golden, endless landscape in the summer and opulent, crusty snow come winter; those summers to savour and winters to endure. Taber, Alberta, with its sweet sugar beets and famous cow corn. Fleeing from this small town life had forever gnawed and tugged at her soul. It was bitter sweet, just like the sweet corn and sugar beets.

Hearing and feeling the rumble of the train approaching, Frances gripped her handbag with a calmness that belied the racing of her heart. She thought of clamouring forward but caught herself in time, wondering if the goodbyes to her family and her friend were sufficient. Since the age of three, as a child prodigy of sorts, she had eagerly read about and anticipated just such an adventure as this. She smiled inwardly as she recalled how she had irritated the librarian, and infuriated her mother with her book-a-day reading habit.

The train seemed poised, magnificently spitting out steam and beckoning to all those who awaited. Frances stood on the worn, wooden platform, desperate to climb aboard. Today was her nineteenth birthday, February 26. The year was 1941, and the country was engulfed in World War ll, an empty, desperate time. The depression in all its brokenness was over. And now there was war, taking loved ones, family members, friend and foe.

Frances was ready to go, but not expecting what her mother was about to give her at this last minute before boarding, before leaving "normal." The outrageous untruth would soon hit her like an unexpected smack in the face. Edith always had remarkable timing. In this moment she was pouting like a child, her lower lip jutting out and quivering, eyes big and mournful, cowering into her fur collared coat. Edith's eyes welled with suspiciously fake tears as she handed Frances her birth certificate, pleading with her to stay. It seemed to be more of a guilty plea, a motherly duty, one could assume. Frances reached out to take the records from her mother's gloved hand, careful not to brush her mother's fingers during the handoff, as touch was not comfortable for either.

Frances glanced down and noticed something amiss. Her name was not there! Instead of seeing the name that she had always gone by emblazoned on the fading paper, another name screamed out at her. The names Mary Frances Lillian Gervais in faded bold font. Mary? When Frances's eyes met her mother's after discovering the fraud, she saw a smirk, a glimmer in her mother's eyes that came from what fed her—a need to lie, a high she got whenever she was caught stretching the truth.

Honesty was not Edith's best policy. Showing no remorse, nor offering an apology or a proper explanation, she instead proffered a villainess-like glare, head tilted back, defiantly looking at Frances down the bridge of her nose. Standing rigid and spitting out her words with a haughty tone, she said, "I never liked the name

Frances. That was your father's idea. Me, I liked the name Mary. It is holy, godly, and in all sense of the word, Catholic!"

As Frances shoved this shocking piece of information into her new navy coloured hand bag (to be examined later) she bit her tongue and closed her purse with such force that she startled even herself. Brushing past Violet to give a briefer than intended hug to sweet Ruth and then embracing her beloved father, Frances climbed up and into her saviour, the locomotive that would take her away from all this, to an exciting new city. A city filled with adventure, love, and new beginnings—Vancouver, British Columbia!

She watched her dad on the platform as her train exhaled, cranking and easing itself away from all that had hurt her. Waving from her seat to the familiar faces, Frances immediately realized that it was her father she would miss the most. Frances saw his pocket watch held firmly in his hand, attached by a long gold chain inside of his vest. He was checking the departure time, as only a station agent would do. Past, present, and future, his first love, and probably his last, were all those things that related to the Station; trains, telegraphs, long journeys, and strangers. Farewell to her father who had done more than just love her. Frances stretched her neck and pressed her face against the window to see him one last time as he waved, mouthing the words, "Bye Billy."

Nestling into her seat, she determined that no tears would be shed, having learned long ago that weeping was not in her vocabulary. Emotion was to be pushed down, unless it was happiness or anger. No tears allowed. Now as they headed west, Frances was not ready to sort through her past. She was not feeling strong enough to look at the soft, folded paper with the name that she did not recognize. Instead Frances found the parcel that Ruth had sheepishly placed into her hand. Ruth's going away present, her way of saying "Farewell, please remember me." Frances smiled as she untied the string and folded back the brown wrapper. Of course, there they were, her favourite store-bought cookies! Frances smiled at Ruth's thoughtfulness.

Frances and Ruth had opposite experiences in their upbringing regarding a mother's role in providing care for the family. When not adorning herself with makeup, Frances's mother spent most of her time baking, canning, stewing, and boiling. These rituals, responsibilities, and time-consuming tasks disgusted Frances. She hated being in the kitchen, as meal preparation and consuming food was not her cup of tea. Frances had no interest (or skill) in standing over a hot stove and then sitting for what seemed like hours over an endless, boring meal. Ruth, however, had grown up without her mother, a woman who was never talked about. Her father raised five children on his own, always settling for store bought baking and pre-canned goods from the local mercantile. As the train picked up speed, Frances anticipated passing by Ruth's family farm.

Gazing out at the windswept prairie, she was reminded of her endless winter and summer activities with Ruth. Sleigh rides and forts in the winter, with sleepovers and homework all year round. During the dry warm days of summer, Frances would ride her bike over to Ruth's farm, helping her with her chores and gobbling down as many packaged cookies as she could. Once in a while they would grab Ruth's bike and together head back to Frances's house. They took their time tootling along the dusty prairie roads, hollering out to empty fields and laughing until they could hardly see straight.

The occasional bully would chase them or throw rocks, but rather than be frightened they were always amused. Frances would happily threaten the taunting culprits with a knuckle sandwich (much to Ruth's horror) in mocking amusement. On one occasion Frances had the bright idea of taking a wet sock and filling it with snow. As she twirled the homemade weapon over her head David and Goliath style, her opponents would flee. Frances was inevitably given the title and reputation of being a Tom Boy. She took the label as a compliment, as only a pure, honest-to-goodness Tom Boy would!

However, her actions and the title that she wore so proudly, were much to her mother's disdain. Frances was the complete antithesis of her mother—plain faced with trousers. Whereas her mother would not show herself in the morning unless she had on a full face of make-up caked on thick like putty, a corset (formally known as Foundation Undergarments) that brought on fainting spells, a dress buttoned to the neck, white gloves to ward off unwanted germs, and of course her polished, buckled up boots. The only visible skin were her ears, which she hated. All this adornment before she set foot in the kitchen to begin her day, would often take three hours to complete the process.

Joe on the other hand, would be fully clothed before Edith, up early to stoke the fire and then hurriedly heading to the attached station to check on the morning telegraphs. Edith really thought she was getting a winner with Joe, his French accent and taste for fine clothes. He was unquestionably a fine catch. From the first time Edith laid eyes on Joe, she knew that she had to have him.

She did not know that shortly after the nuptials of marriage, Joe would become a workaholic, married to his job, his duties, and his love of trains. When Frances came along his world would revolve around her and the station that he managed. Joe and Frances were like two peas in a pod, sharing their love of reading and sports, as well as their frustrations with Edith!

Her thoughts drifted again to her friend. After spending an afternoon at Ruth's house, in imaginative play and adventure, they would arrive at Frances's house, the train station where Frances and her family lived. Often sitting on the platform, legs dangling, dreaming about their futures, Frances dreamed of adventure while Ruth wanted a family and a farm. They were opposite in every sense of the word; appearance, likes and dislikes, and family situations.

ONE THING THEY DID SHARE WAS THEIR LOVE OF BOYS. THEY would giggle about crushes they had, who they could see themselves marrying, and who was worthy to be accepted into their gang. Yes, Frances had a gang! All the waifs and strays from the neighbouring farms would gather every Saturday for mischief and merriment, never causing harm, but liking to think that they could if the opportunity arose.

Just before Ruth would leave Frances's home for her bicycle ride back to the farm, Frances would fill a bag with as much home baking as Ruth could carry. Crusty homemade bread and buns, delectable cookies loaded with chocolate pieces, and jars of her mother's seasonal preserves, were the desired commodities for this secretive affair. Ruth would then head home to make dinner for her brothers and father.

Frances nibbled on her first butter cream store-bought cookie from Ruth while she listened to the relaxing clickety-clack of the train travelling west. As they picked up speed, Frances felt her anticipation and excitement increase at the thoughts of what lay ahead. Putting aside her dream of becoming a private eye, she decided that in the meantime, the practical thing to do was to look for secretarial work. Perhaps after settling in Vancouver she would research detective agencies and start her long awaited career and independence.

Frances visiting Purple Springs

CHAPTER 2

Hitting the Road

It was 1932 in Canada and the United States. The great
Depression had hit. Pulling into the rail yard of a small town
on an early misty morning was a long freight train. Even before
the train came to a complete stop, shadowy figures began
jumping from boxcars to the gravel below. Not five or six but
sixty or more tumbled from the train with small bundles in hand.
Many of their faces were not lined with age; they were the fresh
faces of youth. Many were teenagers – teenagers "on the bum."
They were a part of an army of youthful transients who were
riding the rails. Along the rails the homeless boys and girls
experienced adventure, glimpses of awesome countryside, and
a thrilling sense of freedom. But they also experienced hunger,
danger, boredom, despair, and hostile railroad security guards
known as the "bulls." The life and times of the Great Depression
caused these young people to "hit the road." [3]

POSSESSING BLACK CURLY HAIR, GREEN EYES, AND SUN DRENCHED
skin from working the fields, Vincent Alphonse Bonner went from
a chubby little boy to a tall, dark, and handsome young man in

what seemed like overnight. He was thirteen when he made the decision to leave. Later some would say that he ran away; he would say that he "escaped" if the truth were told, and for story telling purposes he would add, "I left home looking for adventure and business opportunities."

The straw that broke the camel's back was Vince's father Earl's announcement to re-marry. The cleaning lady, (who was not really a cleaning lady at all) was to be Earl's bride. To Vince she was merely a girl. Sixteen-year-old Esther was to be his step mother? Hardly, Vince thought! She was only three years older than himself. Vince had gone to grade school with Esther, in a one room schoolhouse with fourteen students from grade one to grade twelve, though most of the students were lucky to make it to grade seven. To make matters worse, Vince was not fond of Esther in the least. This was seemingly odd for Vince because he liked most people, a flaw that later in life, would turn out to be the best of him and yet the worst of him.

It was the beginning of a new era facing the entire Western World – Europe, Canada, and the United States. The Depression and Prohibition, a time of complete desperation and poverty, would soon be in full swing. It was an era that took hold and engulfed both the urban and rural communities. By 1929 and towards early 1933 many banks had closed, manufacturing had slowed greatly, and millions of people had lost their jobs, money, and homes. Families would experience separation, loss of a homestead, and utter hopelessness that would spread like wild fire. Farmland was dry and barren. Nothing would grow, let alone provide a harvest. This drought would last and linger, driving some to insanity and others to seek solace in the bottle. Broken families exploded, mass hysteria hit the cities, with lost souls on every corner. Men, women, and children were seeking work and finding none, lining the streets from soup kitchen to soup kitchen. Bread lines, depression, and destitution crept in with a vengeance.

The last thing on peoples' minds at this time was their teeth and the cosmetic effects of not having any. Consequently, dentistry was a rare commodity during the late 1920's. Yet here was poor Esther, known for her toothy grin, a mouth filled with gaps, chips, and a noticeable overbite. She could have benefitted from some dentistry. Esther also had an odd way of looking at people, or rather, not looking directly at them at all, her abandoned gaze seeming not quite right. On most occasions she giggled nervously over nothing at all. Most people paid no attention and she was scarcely noticed; neglected, so to speak. Fast forward to the early 1950s and Esther would be labelled as retarded and then much later on as someone with special needs, perhaps Autism or Asperger's. But in the early 1900s there was no such labelling or diagnosis. A little later in the decade, one might commit their child to a sanatorium if they showed signs of being not quite right. Retarded (quite offensive in today's world) was the word that would have been used. Back then in rural Saskatchewan, people just made do with the lot they were given. To Vince she appeared half-witted, or rather, "not having a lot upstairs" as he told it, a real odd ball. His feelings were only magnified by the upcoming nuptials between Esther and his father. Esther sixteen, and Earl thirty two, exactly sixteen years her senior, were to be married at the end of harvest, if there was one. This was one wedding that Vince would not be attending.

VINCE'S UNCLE CHUCK WAS ALWAYS COMING UP WITH A GET-RICH-quick scheme, but nothing ever came of these ventures, until he got word that another farm (one of many) had gone belly up and everything given back to the bank. Chuck decided to head over to the farm to look around. Having the gift of the gab, he struck up a conversation with another farmer. While engrossed in the conversation, Chuck noticed a SOLD sign on a brand spanking new Model T Ford. Noticing some men wearing fancy suits, he inquired about the vehicle, and discovered the car needed to be transported to Vancouver. A rich fellow there had purchased it sight unseen.

Chuck's wheels started turning, and without thinking too much about it, he blurted out that he was planning a trip out west, and for a fee he would be happy to deliver the car. Everyone shook hands and Chuck was promised $100.00 upon delivery. This is how he happened to agree to drive Vince west to the land of opportunity.

Vince and his Uncle Chuck drove all night. The Model T Ford was as reliable as the newspaper and radio commercials promised. The engine purred as they made their way along the dusty prairie road from Bengough, Saskatchewan to Calgary, Alberta. This road seemed to go on forever, leaving the travellers not knowing when, or if, they would reach their destination, due to lack of funds and never having made the trip before. It was a road less travelled, leaving another world behind like the closing of a story book, a tall tale, or a nightmare, with only a happy ending on the horizon. There was hardly a bend, twist, or turn in the road, making it so easy to lose themselves in the monotony of the dull, never changing scenery.

Dry winds whirled among the brittle tumbleweeds, through each passing farm, and the empty, deserted homesteads that followed eerily one after another. The small, empty one-horse towns were few and far between. Corner stores, cafes, and gas pumps, once thriving establishments, were only the outer shell and memory of profitable days gone by.

The fresh faced, smiling girl on the Coca Cola sign now wore a look of sad betrayal. Her fresh, rosy cheeks and blonde curls offered a rusty and tarnished hue. Vince, having never before left his own small town, was getting a glimpse of the devastation that came with the 1930s. The roaring '20s had aimlessly, yet hurriedly turned into the bleak dirty '30s.

Vince's Uncle Chuck, always rugged and coarse-grained, continued to nurse his bottle of Jack Daniels throughout the drive heading west. Sometimes he would pull over to let Vince take the wheel. More often than not, Chuck's determination to uphold his end of the deal, fuelled him to push through and past his sleepy, drunken haze. Vince would not allow his Uncle's habitual state to squelch his feelings of hope. Hope for a better life, a new beginning. Anything was an improvement to the life he was leaving behind. His optimism was open-ended, innocent, and forever changing with each passing mile.

As fatigue encompassed Vince, thoughts of chicken and dumplings, homemade lemon meringue pie, and rows upon rows of garden fresh vegetables filled his mind with dream-like visions. Food was a huge priority for Vince. It was also a rare commodity and hard to come by. Money had always been scarce and without mother's tender, loving hands to skilfully prepare such staples, Vince often hankered for a better life. It was a common occurrence to long for his next meal while he drifted into sleep each night.

On this night as they pulled over to camp on the side of the road, Vince drifted into a fitful sleep, thinking of the comfort of his iron four poster bed. Dreams of sticky, sweet hot cross buns intertwined with wakeful memories of events surrounding food, or the lack of it, back in the little clapboard shack in Bengough. Vince, his father, brother, and uncles, had lived on potatoes and eggs for as far back as he could remember. The school lunches that Vince and brother Hank would muster up and take turns preparing, were dismal and grey, except for one occasion a few months before, when it was Vince's turn to fill the metal pail with a mid-day meal of leftovers that would sustain himself and his brother at school. Vince remembered that for dinner the night before, they had been delighted with Uncle George's hot cakes.

Someone had brought home a bag of flour, brown sugar, and a one-pound rectangular block of lard, very scarce items, almost unheard of. Combined with eggs from the hen house and water from the pump, a meal fit for a king was fried up in the skillet, a cast iron frying pan. They ate the crispy-edged, doughy hot cakes for supper until their bellies were bursting. Thrilled to find enough hotcakes left over, Vince prepared the lunches with joy that morning, thinking of how he often felt weary from envy and nagging jealousy when sitting next to classmates with bright, fleshy oranges and sandwiches overflowing with ham and an abundance of cheese, lathered with mustard on fresh sour dough bread. This day would be different.

On this day Vince had risen early. The syrup they had made last night with the brown sugar and water, had been boiled to a sweet and runny consistency, perfect for drizzling. Alternating hot cake, syrup, hot cake, syrup, hot cake, Vince filled the tin lunch bucket to 3/4 of the way full. To finish off the eye-pleasing feast, Vince placed ten hardboiled eggs on top of the entire stack of hot cakes, secured the lid firmly and ran out the door to begin the two-mile trek to school. He could hardly wait to see the look on his brother's face when the lunch bell rang. Maybe there would be some jealous stares in his direction for a change.

When the 12:00 noon cow bell chimed, Vince could not wipe the grin of anticipation from his face. Urgently walking to the cloak room, he scrambled to take out his awaited treasure. To his horror and utter dismay Vince discovered that the eggs had sunk down into the hot cakes, ending up at the bottom of the pail. The hotcakes had combined with the syrup to create a mess, a thick doughy, mushy mixture resembling pig mash. Only the eggs were edible. Once again Vince had to face his brother Hank's wrath. In the darkness of the prairie night, huddled in the back of the Ford, Vince now physically cringed at the thought of the botched lunch he had tried so hard to make nice. Hank was gentle and kind to most, but with Vince he was always exasperated and annoyed.

As he struggled to sleep, Vince thought of his father Earl, who had come by the title of town drunk, and rightly so, along with many others. To Vince the entire town was filled with drunkards and home wreckers. Thinking back, he could not fathom any other way to be but poor, and longing for a better life. Earl drank on a regular basis, a happy drunk and a mean drunk, nothing in between. Vince would wonder on more than one occasion why the need to drink to oblivion? What did people see in the bitter, putrid liquid? Alcohol was the catalyst to his whole predicament. The sufferings of poverty came second to the evils and abuse that liquor brought.

Thoughts came of the upcoming nuptials between Esther and Earl, and rather than being saddened, Vince was repulsed and disgusted. His lifetime of sadness had faded years ago, evolving into a dull pain that Vince endured daily. His heart had been broken, and the effort of continually trying to mend it had left well-worn grooves. He felt like he could never be capable of loving or feeling the warmth and presence of a living thing. It was like a precious antique vase that had been flung against a wall, shattered and then carelessly glued back together, unable to hold water, let alone the flowers that represented fresh life, fresh beauty. Flowers eventually die, as do people, he thought. And people go away, or turn their backs, leaving you to grow and bloom on your own, then to die and turn to dust, to be blown away in the harsh, unforgiving wind.

Long before the wedding of Esther and Earl, there had been another wedding, a wedding between Vince's mother and his father. It was somewhat of a shot gun wedding, but a wedding nevertheless. Vince's mother Martha was a faded, distant memory. She had gone, leaving behind himself, his brother Henry, and their father, taking with her his two sisters, baby Bonnie and big sister Geneva. Both girls were dark haired beauties. Geneva was a fire cracker, with high energy and high cheek bones, raven curls, and ruby red lips; a real livewire. Bonnie was sweet and demure, petite, with the same olive skin as Vince's, and close-set round eyes that sparkled with mischief.

Bonnie was the baby of the family. Next was Vince, then Hank, with the eldest being Geneva. Abruptly, mother and two sisters were gone, moved away to another town perhaps. Not even a goodbye. Rumour had it that they had relocated to the United States of America. Who knew where they had settled? Vince's biological mother Martha was a strong and stoic woman. She was large boned, a rugged beauty with a permanent scowl that could freeze a hot prairie August night. Her loving arms would embrace a child so tightly they would rather stay and die in the strong hold than be let go.

Martha and Earl made an odd couple. Vince's father was a wiry little man with hair like steel wool, much like a character out of a story book. Earl (before the drink got the better of him) told stories, danced, and sang. Later he was known to drink moonshine until there was not a drop left in the jug or even in the town. He was a prankster whose jokes were comical to everyone but Vince. After the alcohol took hold, his jokes turned mean and hurtful, with what seemed like endless teasing.

Vince's mother ultimately decided to leave Vince and Hank, who were five and seven at the time, alone with their father and two uncles. Was it the drink, the incessant arguing, or the violence and poverty that forced her away, Vince often wondered? Or was it him? Had he done or said something to send her away? Vince endlessly went over the events each night as he lay down to sleep. There were no longer any comforting nightly prayers or fresh cotton sheets, no bedtime snacks or warm milk to soothe his little boy needs.

A TATTERED DRESS THAT BELONGED TO HIS MOTHER WAS THE ONLY tangible object left behind. It was worn and old, the polka dots having seen better days. He held the dress as he cried himself to sleep on a nightly basis. Later the dress was taken from his grasp while he slept one night. His attachment to his mother's discarded clothing embarrassed brother Hank and the uncles. It was pointed out to Vince that only a baby would sleep cuddling a frayed, shoddy dress. The only remnant to have and to hold of his mother's was now gone, buried out in the godforsaken prairie. She never returned. The era of depression in the 1930s eventually chased every breath of life away from Bengough, Saskatchewan. Many years later, as an adult Vince would look for the town, his birth place on a map, only to find there was no record of Bengough. It was completely gone, wiped right off the map.

"Abandoned Child Syndrome" is a behavioural or psychological condition that results primarily from the loss of one or both parents. Abandonment may be physical, as in the parent is not present in the child's life, or emotional in that the parent withholds affection, nurturing, or basic care-giving.

Child abandonment occurs when a parent, guardian, or person in charge of a child deserts a child or fails to provide necessary care for a child living under the same roof.

These early-childhood experiences can lead to a fear of being abandoned by the significant people in one's adult life. When a child has abandonment issues their moods and symptoms can be feelings of insecurity, depression, decreased self-esteem, feelings of loss or control over their life, self-deprecation, isolation, obsessive thinking and intrusive thoughts about the abandonment. [4]

As the Model T sat quietly on the side of the road, Vince was abruptly awakened by Uncle Chuck's jostling. It was time to hit the road again. Leaving his dreams and the realities of his past behind, silencing the thoughts and voices ringing in his ears and clouding his mind, Vince gathered himself to be present and in the moment. In less than a week he would be in the province where food was easy to come by, jobs were on every corner, and lush forests and vegetable gardens engulfed every home!

British Columbia, the land of opportunity. Even the name sounded royal and rich. "The province's name was chosen by Queen Victoria in 1858, reflecting its origins as the British remainder of the Columbia District of the Hudson's Bay Company." [5] Happy and healthy B.C. was the westernmost province of Canada, located between the Pacific Ocean and the Rocky Mountains. There, Vince would start a new life. He would find his way.

Vince would always remember the plan, the course of action – leaving in the middle of the night. Sixty dollars, a fortune to Vince, was pinned inside of his long johns underneath his trousers to keep it safe. The well-thought-out plan was that, upon reaching Calgary, Vince and his uncle would climb aboard the box car and Vince would begin his journey. He would block out and forget his past, and his frightening and lonely existence. Vince did not know that the unbridled fear, torment, and suffering of his childhood would forever haunt him. He would be marked for life, like an ugly mole or a regretted tattoo, continuously pushing down his pain, only for it to rise up periodically at the least opportune times.

Gazing out the dusty window as the Model T Ford rattled on towards their destination, Vince thought of his uncles, drunk Uncle Chuck, and mean Uncle George. His father Earl and his uncles were all hard workers, but when there was no work to be done during the depression, the idle days brought boredom, animosity, and raw nerves. The alcohol only exacerbated the problem.

Vince sharply recalled a recent event that only added more scars to the shame and humiliation of his childhood. This new trauma was another catalyst that led to his decision to leave. He had been sent out into a dark and stormy night to retrieve the eggs from the barn. Why it could not wait until morning, he did not know! The wind whistled and ran along the prairie like a thick black demon that autumn night, engulfing everything in its path. As it was impossible to see, Vince went by feel, relying on his memory of the land, and the layout of the barn. Shaking with the cold, Vince hurriedly searched under each hen, quickly snatching the two or three eggs from each, and filling the tin pail. Unbeknownst to Vince, his Uncle George was hiding in the darkness behind the old, broken barn door. Barely hanging from its hinges, the door flapped and banged in the night, adding to the fear that Vince was feeling. From his hiding spot, Uncle George grasped a rusty chain in one hand and an old metal bucket in the other. Just as Vince was completing his task, George began rattling the chain inside the bucket, letting out an atrocious, blood-curdling roar. Frightened to death, Vince dropped the egg bucket and ran for his life, certain he was being followed by some terrible monster. Every last egg lay broken on the dusty barn floor, now painted a bright yellow by the yolks. As he ran, his uncle's hoarse laugh was deafening in his ears, only to be joined by that of his father and brother as he blasted through the door and ran straight to his bed.

As the flat brown plains meandered into greener valleys, Uncle Chuck announced, "We're gettin' close boy, that'd be Swift Current jus' on yonder there. In about six or seven hours, we'll be entering the booming township of Calgary, Alberta, the legendary hub of horses and cattle ranching!" His Uncle's announcement broke into Vince's thoughts, his anger from his flashback abruptly dissipating.

With the vehicle exiting the main thoroughfare at Swift Current, they would fuel up and hopefully find some cheap food that would carry them all the way through to British Columbia. Vince and Uncle Chuck were both famished to say the least, and entirely wiped out. Vince had been keeping his eye on both the road and his uncle, while securely gripping the money pinned on the inside of his trousers. This concentration, along with always being in a relentless state of recollection, was tiring. Chuck was weary from driving while sipping his booze on an empty stomach, concentrating on the endless, narrow, and desolate road, dry-eyed and peering straight ahead. It was 11:00 a.m. and time for lunch.

Uncle Chuck spotted Molly's Diner. The sign on the window promised home cooked meals by Molly herself, guaranteed to leave you satisfied. "Can't beat that," exclaimed Uncle Chuck. Having never been too far away from home, the adventure of sitting down, ordering a meal, and having it brought to you was fascinating and exciting for Vince.

Red leather seats, cutlery, sugar, and salt and pepper shakers on every table were an utter amazement to Vince. They chose a booth because, as Uncle Chuck put it, "No one needs to know our business, that's what these booths are made for—privacy." Over lunch, Chuck wanted to discuss the plan with Vince, of getting to the train station, manoeuvring the Model T up onto the ramp, bracing it down on the flat deck of the train, then finding their way to an empty box car for the twenty-hour journey west.

A vibrant blue-eyed, red-headed waitress approached the table with menus in hand. She wore a crisp, pink uniform, starched white apron and displayed a name tag that read **GLORIA** in bold letters. Vince had heard about Hollywood actors and actresses and after meeting Gloria he figured that he had rightfully come across a genuine movie star!

Vince had never met someone so friendly, exuberant, and beautifully dressed. Not only that, Gloria smiled warmly with eyes that were inviting and kind. Quite a contrast to what now felt like the ancient history of Vince's past! Gloria was now offering to bring them fresh water and hot coffee, even before they had paid! This to Vince was sheer luxury.

Gloria recited the Blue Plate Special of fried liver and onions, mashed potatoes and gravy, a thick slice of Molly's homemade sour dough bread slathered with butter, and raisin pie for dessert—a delightfully sweet sound to Vince's ears. "What? That's it that for fifty cents each?" hollered Uncle Chuck. "Mighty steep if you ask me, but we are on a holiday, so bring us the works, sweetheart."

Off went Gloria to retrieve their food, sashaying back to the kitchen to place their order.

Never, ever had Vince been tended to, cared for, and nurtured by such a dazzling woman; a rather heady enterprise and one he would never forget. Thus began Vince's love of waitresses. For the rest of his lifetime he would always value waitressing. The job ranked high on his priority list as a well-deserved, respected way to make a living.

Throughout the meal, Uncle Chuck reminded Vince of all the pitfalls in riding the rails. First and foremost, it was illegal, and secondly, awfully dangerous. "You can get thrown off without a moment's notice," said Uncle Chuck. "Keep your head down, don't talk to no one and most importantly, do not leave my side. Don't worry kid, everyone's doing it these days, and everybody's got a right to a fresh start." Looking at this man, his father's brother, Vince now saw a unique kindness. Rough and rugged on the outside, and all heart on the inside. At that precise moment, in the booth of Molly's diner, at thirteen years old, Vince decided that Uncle Chuck was a good ole sod, aside from his enslavement to the hard stuff. Alcohol was to blame for all cruelty, in Vince's mind.

After the meal Uncle Chuck picked up the tab and they proceeded to the dry goods mercantile across the street, purchasing some dried beef, black liquorice and two bottles of Coca Cola, chewing tobacco, and some Sen-Sen.

JUST BEHIND THE GENERAL STORE, COINCIDENTALLY, THERE appeared to be a shack, a homespun distillery, boasting the finest moonshine made from the purest form of Idaho potatoes. Chuck told Vince to take the supplies to the car and he would join him momentarily. This put Vince on guard. A foreboding crept into Vince's senses, and the alarm bells began to sound in his ears. It was the same feeling he had felt many times before, the feeling that something lurked in the shadows to take away his joy, his hope, his faith in better times ahead.

Sen-Sen was a type of breath freshener originally marketed as a "breath perfume.' Sen-Sen's distinctive, strong scent, was popular during the 1930's to the 1950's. Its purpose was covering up the odoriferous evidence of perceived vices such as drinking and cigarette smoking. Sen-Sen was formerly made by Ernest Jackson & company, Ltd. Available in small packets or cardboard boxes similar to a matchbox of the time, an inner box slid out from a cardboard sleeve revealing a small hole. Shaking the box would release the tiny Sen-Sen squares. [6]

Alcohol; fermented grain, vegetables, fruit juice, plants and honey have been used to make alcohol (ethyl alcohol or ethanol) for thousands of years.

In India, a beverage called Sura, distilled from rice, was an alcoholic drink dating back between 3000 and 2000 B.C. Fermented beverages existed in China and in the early Egyptian civilization around 7000 B.C. The Babylonians worshipped a wine goddess as early as 2700 B.C. In Greece one of the first alcoholic beverages to gain popularity was mead, a fermented drink made from water and honey. In South America in the region of the Andes, a fermented beverage known as "Chica" was made from corn, grapes or apples.

In the sixteenth century, alcohol, was signified as "spirits" and was used as medicine in what was thought of as healing tonics. In the eighteenth century the British Parliament passed a law encouraging the use of grain for distilling spirits. Cheap liquor flooded the market and reached a peak in the mid-18th century. In Britain alone gin consumption reached eighteen million gallons and alcoholism became widespread.

The 19th century brought a change in attitude. The violence and breakdown of the family was the beginning of the temperance movement which in turn promoted the moderate use of alcohol, which ultimately became the push for total prohibition.

It was in 1920 that the U.S. passed a law prohibiting the manufacture, sale, import and export of intoxicating liquors. Today an estimated fifteen million North Americans suffer from alcoholism and forty percent of all car deaths involve alcohol. [7]

Back in the car, they were now hustling down the barren road west to downtown Calgary and the train yard. Vince had noticed the brown burlap sack that Chuck had carried out to the car and placed in the rumble seat. Clanking mason jars soon brought the realization that all was not well. Aside from the moonshine purchase, Vince felt momentarily brightened from his café meal, thinking about Gloria's goodness and the prospect of something new on the horizon.

The journey that they were about to embark on meant something different to each of them. After this job of delivering the Model T to its new owner, Chuck was aiming to knuckle down. Perhaps do a little freelance, nine to five, be gainfully employed. He had high hopes that his life as he knew it in Saskatchewan was going to change. Change for the better. He would settle down in British Columbia, and he would send for his brother Earl and his bride Esther, his nephew Hank, and his other brother George. They would all establish themselves somewhere and have a fine life. Vince felt he had bigger fish to fry, find a town, get a job and make it rich. Maybe someday he would own a restaurant or coffee shop of his own, serving homemade pie, with a pretty waitress like Gloria. A thirteen-year-old boy's simple, yet hopeful plan, one that was fleeting and would change like the variable coastal weather.

As THEY PULLED INTO THE TRAIN STATION THERE SEEMED TO BE confusion all around. People, livestock, vehicles, trolleys, luggage and baggage carriers were all scrambling to find their place. They were instructed to purchase their tickets and proceed to the cargo area where the Model T Ford would be driven up onto the flat deck of the train.

Following the procession, and with much determination, they were able to drive the car up a ramp which consisted of only two 4 x 4's; nerve racking to Vince but do-able to Chuck. Once the car was in place and secured with a block of wood under each wheel, when all attention was elsewhere, Chuck and Vince slipped around the other side and walked the length of the train, figuring out where the best spot would be to climb aboard. What they did not know was that every box car would be either locked or filled with livestock, vehicles, and household material. Chuck, being the sly, dodgy fellow that he was, had another idea. They would climb up on top of the train and ride there.

At the mention of this new plan Vince was terrified and reluctant to follow his uncle. But, being the age he was, inexperience and naivety would get the better of him, and he soon began to climb the narrow three-runged ladder. Ascending to the roof of the boxcar, to Vince's amazement he saw that there were already dozens of other men, teenagers, and boys who had done the same thing.

Vince felt relieved to know that they had company. Safety in numbers assured that they were okay, doing the right, necessary thing. Surely these adults would take care of him if need be. Unfortunately, Vince was wrong. It was every man for himself. In the midst of extreme poverty and near starvation most humans behave differently than they would in another, more comfortable and civilized situation. Within Uncle Chuck's tight grip, lock stock and barrel, they were off.

The wheels began to crank slowly, with ear-piercing squeals coming from metal on metal. The steam let out a putrid smell of burning coal as people lobbied for a secure foothold on top of the boxcar. Vince sat tight, holding on for dear life. Praying. Even though he knew in his heart that there was no God, he prayed as if there was.

As he had done many times before, Vince questioned the God that most feared. If there was a God then why would he allow a thirteen-year-old boy to be in this place, why would his mother leave him, why would he need to leave his home searching for freedom? Vince remembered a time when Evangelists came to town, putting up signs—The Lord is coming! Repent! Repent!" Signs advertising a revival meeting—"Save your souls, let Jesus give you a new life, a better life. Be washed clean and be born again."

Vince was a mere seven years old at the time. It was only two years after his mother had left with his sisters Bonnie and Geneva. Feeling abruptly alone, with no rhyme or reason, it was then that Vince began to fervently search for solace and some form of love. Could it be in this Jesus fellow that the whole town was talking about? Some scoffed, but many were light hearted at the prospect that these circuit riders brought.

The tents were raised, almost like a big-top circus. "Saturday, meet at the tents and Jesus will save you. All your pain, fear, and suffering will be wiped away. Freedom, praise Jesus, freedom." This message was belted out from megaphones. Posters also declared the coming of the Lord, harbingers announcing from soap boxes throughout the small, desperate town.

Vince felt bewildered, yet hopeful and somewhat elated that perhaps, just maybe this Jesus chum could help him. With no money in his pockets he could not afford a ticket to get inside the large canvas tent but what he could afford was to get his knuckles rapped as he lay on his belly and peeked under the side.

He saw crying and hollering, people fainting and falling to their knees, shaking, gyrating and singing with hands raised. He thought that they had all gone mad, stark raving mad. He ran home as fast as his legs would carry him, sobbing and stumbling. Picking himself up and swallowing down his tears, he wiped his face and let the anger and frustration build at the cruelty of it all. Where was this Jesus that they all spoke so highly of?

Jolted from his thoughts as the train picked up speed, Vince was instantly brought back to present-day. The bodies lay row upon row. "Do not sit up or stand up" was shouted from all directions. "If you want to make it to the end of the line, stay down!" someone else hollered. The bitter, chilly wind cut through Vince's skin. His shivering helped to keep him warm. The strangers that were crammed up against him were a blessing and a curse. The smell of stale alcohol, the stench of unwashed bodies, and the added warmth from human contact was all-encompassing.

As the locomotive approached the spectacular Rocky Mountains, while Vince sat braced and shivering on top of the box cars, continuous warnings rang out.

Thick, heavy duty cables intending to clear off the snow from the top of each box car hung down at the mouth of every tunnel. If a body sat or stood at the wrong moment, they too would be cleared off as easily as the wind blowing a leaf from a tree. At one point Vince felt a massive weight being flung down on top of him.

Afraid to open his eyes he just gripped more tightly onto the body next to him. Later he realized that someone had thrown an old straw filled mattress, the kind from a discarded bed frame, on top of him and those around him.

The mattress protected them from the rain inside the tunnels and prevented bewildered or disoriented riders from standing. The tattered, mouldy mattress was intended to keep them safe from the dangling cables as they hung down and tore across into the box spring, creating loose threads and flying straw. The frozen, icy drops of water that fell from the pitch-dark caverns were absorbed into the mattress, creating more weight. Inadvertently staying warm and dry, Vince faded in and out of a fear induced sleep and unconsciousness.

The old homestead

The Model T Ford

Vince, Hank,
Ma, GiGi, Pa,
Baby Bonnie

Two-year-old Vince,
Four-year-old Hank

CHAPTER 3

New Beginnings

RAIN, RAIN GO AWAY, COME AGAIN............ NEVER!!

> Vancouver, British Columbia is Canada's third most
> rainy city, with over 161 rainy days per year. As measured at
> Vancouver Airport in Richmond, Vancouver receives 1,153.1
> mm (45.40 in) of rain per year.
>   By comparison, the amount of rainfall in London, England
> is nearly half that of Vancouver. [8]

Excited to be arriving in Vancouver after a long train ride, Frances was not prepared for the dark skies and endless rain. Now understanding the term "It's raining cats and dogs," she found herself thinking "How on earth could Noah stand rain for 40 days and 40 nights as the Bible rightly taught me so?!"

Recollecting her recent journey from Taber, Alberta, immediately brought back fond memories. The warm cosy berth and thick wool blankets were a comfort to Frances. The soap in her soap dish, and the fluffy white hand towel instantly brought back the aroma of ivory soap. Every summer for the past ten years, during the late '20s and early '30s, Frances had travelled east to

Montreal by train. Partly because of her father's employment with
the railway and partly because of her love of adventure and travel,
Frances would beg until they would let her go. She rode for free
and had many uncles and aunties that she adored, waiting to show
her a good time.

As the train began to slow down with the rain descending
outside, a foggy, barely memorable thought crept into Frances's
mind—an unsettling flashback. Within her thoughts of Montreal
came the reflection of her older twin uncles, two men that she
loathed. Something happened to her on one of her trips out east,
something to be pushed down and erased from her mind forever.
She couldn't quite remember the scene but felt shame and heat on
her face as she reluctantly tried to conjure up what took place on
one of her trips. Frances instinctively knew in her heart, her reality
of being a young woman, that whatever happened back then was
not good. It was worth blocking. Choosing not to fret about the
incident was all Frances could do, all she must do, while waiting
for her Vancouver taxi cab to arrive, the motor vehicle that would
carry her safely to her new destination—Miss Sylvia's Boarding
House for Young Women in Shaughnessy, a very well-to-do part
of Vancouver.

> Shaughnessy is an almost entirely residential neighbourhood
> in Vancouver, British Columbia, Canada, spanning about
> 447 hectares in a relatively central location. It was named
> after Thomas Shaughnessy, 1st Baron Shaughnessy, former
> president of the Canadian Pacific Railway. The neighbourhood
> was created in 1907 by the Canadian Pacific Railway, then
> the largest real estate developer in Canada. Shaughnessy is
> known for its elegant tree-lined streets and large properties. [9]

Frances marvelled at the high pink and gold ceilings of the
Vancouver train station. The interior architecture reminded

her of Montreal, which gave her a remote feeling of nostalgia. Vancouver, in comparison, was a much younger city, incomparable to the astute beauty of the Notre-Dame Basilica built in 1829, the City Hall, or St. James United Church. But still, apart from her immediate introduction to the luminous rain, Frances loved Vancouver already.

A SHINY BLACK TAXI CAB WAS RIGHT OUTSIDE THE STATION waiting for Frances as she emerged from the heavy-duty brass doors. Although she had never taken a taxi cab before, Frances had seen enough Clark Gable movies at her local movie theatre to know exactly what to do. It was all rather romantic, as the driver carefully placed her bags in the trunk. Frances climbed in the back seat, almost expecting a tall dark stranger to join her.

Inside the cab, the sound of the rain continued. The rhythm on the roof of the cab was like a melody to Frances; music that would eventually, months from now, turn into the droning beat of an unwanted drum, never ceasing, never letting in clarity for thoughts to flourish. The blue skies and bright light of sunshine that Frances took for granted in her small Prairie town were seemingly non-existent in this new silver and blue city. The light of day that fed her mental state, enhancing her mood and state of mind, was now absent. Never until now had Frances realised the glory of sunrise to sunset and its all-encompassing importance.

As the taxi cab wound through the streets of Vancouver, Frances was somewhat enlightened by the sights and sounds of the Pacific Ocean, the Burrard Street Bridge, Kitsilano, and then Jericho Beach. She felt breathless at what lay ahead.

Taking in the spectacular setting, Frances was momentarily brought back to her recent journey; the gradual removal from the past while traversing towards the future. Stretching out in her compartment on the train, Frances had soaked up the scenery like she was doing now. Never having travelled west before, the Rocky Mountains took her breath away, just as the expansive beach was doing now, but in a different way. The mountains were majestic and surreal as the train had passed through Banff, Alberta and on to Golden, B.C. Photographs did not do justice to the towering, jagged razor blades of rock jutting out of the mountainside, or to powerful, long horn sheep, massive moose peacefully grazing, and brave bald-headed eagles soaring high, looking for their next prey. Now this new landscape, the city outside her taxi window, was twinkling and glistening, calling to her for adventure and new beginnings.

With travel comes weariness, with fatigue comes hunger. Frances had truly enjoyed her meals on the train. Amongst the comforts of fresh linen table cloths, white china dishes, and impeccably kind service, Frances felt like she had died and gone to heaven. Her favourite food for breakfast was a strawberry Danish. Crisp, fluffy pastry with gooey strawberry jam filling the centre, topped with sugary white icing; egg salad sandwiches (even though she despised mayonnaise) for lunch, and a choice of roasted chicken or smoked trout for dinner. She felt like the Queen of England, not knowing that one day soon she would stand in a long line of patriots to meet, or rather, wave at her Royal Highness.

The further Frances was removed from her childhood home and memories, the more her appetite picked up speed, like coal being shuffled into the ravenous coal car. Frances had decided on Ruth's store-bought cookies for dinner and an early night with her new book, _Gone With The Wind_, by Margaret Mitchell.

The taxi continued to carefully manoeuvre its way through slick, rain drenched streets, eventually dropping Frances off at the women's boarding house promptly at six o'clock p.m.

MISS SYLVIA GAVE FRANCES A DETAILED TOUR OF THE ROOMING house and read her the riot act as she stood with bags in hand, dripping onto the plastic runners in the hallway. Frances quickly noticed that there was plastic everywhere. Bright transparent plastic covered the furniture, the hallway carpets, and glistened all the way up the stairs. Even her bed mattress underneath the sheets was covered in yellowing plastic. Nothing worse than the crinkling sound underneath while trying to sleep, the cold, slippery feel on one's bare legs while trying to get comfortable. How would she ever sleep? Not one for fretting or even sleeping for that matter, Frances knew that a hot bath and an enjoyable book would cure her feelings of...of what, she was not quite sure. It certainly can't be homesickness, Frances thought. Was it hope or foreboding? Perhaps a little of both she decided.

Frances was brought back to attention as Miss Sylvia cleared her throat and droned on about the house rules and regulations. Noting this aggressive little woman, Frances was taken aback by the round face and bristly chin of Miss Sylvia. A true-blue honest to goodness spinster. Perhaps back in the day of stage coaches and schoolmarms, Miss Sylvia could have been quite a looker. Now greying with tight pin curls adorning her head and a sausage-like corset underneath a floral house dress, Miss Sylvia showed signs of aging, with an agitated disposition, seemingly alone and desperate for respect. Transfixed by Miss Sylvia's upper lip moving like a bleating Billy Goat, something green wedged between her front teeth and a spit bubble starting to form in the corner of her mouth, Frances thought that Miss Sylvia resembled a dowdy version of what her own mother would have looked like had she not married, or rather if she hadn't snagged Frances's father and all his money.

No sooner than it had started, the monologue had ended, and Frances found herself alone in her new room. "Tomorrow, job hunting, but first, bath, bed, and book," Frances caught herself exclaiming out loud.

Up bright and early, Frances skipped breakfast and the possibility of Miss Sylvia's lamenting, making her way out the door of the boarding house and before long to the streetcar. Still raining. Frances didn't care. Today was her day and as on the big screen of the local movie theatre, Frances hopped aboard the cable car and with a "ding, ding" she was off.

Vancouver Electric Railway and Light Company Limited launched Vancouver's streetcar system on June 27 1890. Westminster and Vancouver Tramway Company launched New Westminster's streetcar system on October 8 1891 as well as the Vancouver – New Westminster interurban line (via Central Park in Burnaby) in the same year. In 1890 all three companies went into receivership and were amalgamated. On May 26 1896 one of the worst transit disasters in British Columbia history occurred in Victoria. A streetcar, loaded over capacity with 143 passengers on their way to attend celebrations of Queen Victoria's birthday, crashed through Point Ellice Bridge into the upper harbour. Fifty-five men, women and children were killed in the accident. Only passengers on the left side of the streetcar escaped.

The Consolidated Electric Railway was forced into receivership by the disaster and re-emerged in 1897 coining the new company name of B.C. Electric. The Streetcar and Interurban electric railway system in southwestern British Columbia ran primarily in greater Vancouver, North Vancouver, New Westminster, Burnaby, Surrey, Langley, Abbotsford, Chilliwack, Deep Cove, Richmond, North Saanich, Saanich, Esquimalt, and Victoria until the trolleys were discontinued in 1958, being replaced with bus and trolley bus systems. These lines subsequently became part of BC Transit and the routes in greater Vancouver eventually came under the control of Translink. [10]

Needing to pick up some essentials, Frances disembarked from the street car at Steadman's, the local five and dime store on Granville Street. Steadman's was a popular store in Lethbridge as well. Frances knew exactly what she needed for the day to be a success. Upon entering the store, Frances had a little sit down on a stool at the soda fountain. A large white counter top had groupings of catsup and sugar containers, salt and pepper shakers, and napkin holders, dispersed in a nice neat format. A refreshing orange float would fill Frances's belly almost as nicely as a sugary strawberry Danish. A breakfast to live and die for—sugar, Frances's best friend and worst enemy.

Next on her list was a mandatory purchase of an umbrella, a newspaper, a diary, rouge, and lipstick. Because her mother concealed herself in makeup, Frances always preferred not to wear any, but a big city girl needed to look the part, and her new image went with her new "smart lady" persona. The latest movie magazines depicted Betty Davis and Joan Crawford in ruby red lipstick, high cheek bones with streaks of rogue, and a tight cinched in waist. Frances knew that with her height and pale complexion she could certainly pull off a similar look, not quite as confident as the movie stars from the silver screen, but certainly willing and able.

If Mother and Violet could only see her now, Frances thought. She pictured her mother gasping and Violet rolling her eyes at her newfound city girl image. Taking a moment to briefly miss Ruth, Frances opened the Vancouver Sun, and all thoughts of her family and best friend vanished.

Her first job interview was for a taxidermist situated down on Main Street and Terminal. Walking from Granville to Main and left on Terminal, Frances found the address that she was looking for. It was a longer walk than she had anticipated, but a great way to learn more about the city.

First impression—"horrifying" would be the term to describe Frances's thoughts upon entering the Taxidermy. Rigid stuffed owls on ledges, dusty bats hanging from the ceiling, and even a chipmunk tied to the ceiling fan, or perhaps it was a flying squirrel; cats and an assortment of birds, while off in the corner a rather large bear stared into the dark overcrowded shop. Before Frances could hand off her resume to the small, beady-eyed balding man across the counter, she was spooked and repulsed by her surroundings. It was not a total surprise when the beady-eyed balding man leaned over and nonchalantly patted Frances on her bottom. As the repulsive little man winked and smirked, Frances so wanted to slap him across the face, Lana Turner style. Instead, she made an immediate about face and retreated to the now revitalizing, yet still dreary rain. As it pelted down around her, Frances exclaimed out loud, to no one in particular, "That is one job I can do without."

The days turned into weeks and the weeks turned into months, still no job and still buckets of rain. Miss Sylvia kept ranting on assorted topics daily and Frances started to display a slight heaviness of stature, as she was not standing quite as tall anymore. The dark clouds seemed to be clouding her brain in addition to the grey skies. Her enthusiasm for her new city was beginning to diminish. Thinking about the change in her mood, she tried to figure out why. Frances knew that it was not because she missed her home life, because she didn't, although she did have a slight foreboding when she first got off the train months earlier, and she did continuously dream about the clear, opulent blue skies of Taber and those endless days of clarity. Frances tried to keep in mind what had brought her here to the coast, to the province of opportunity. For years, she had always had a plan, what seemed like a lifelong dream, to come west. Now all she could think about was missing the weather and her dear friend Ruth. She knew that she had to push through this detour, this slight delay in starting her new life.

Seasonal Bipolar Disorder. The change in season can trigger mood changes in some people with bipolar disorder. Spring and summer may trigger symptoms of mania or hypomania, while the onset of fall and winter can bring on symptoms of depression. Light helps your body to produce serotonin which is your body's mood enhancer. Sunlight and exercise are great ways to increase serotonin.

Physical and emotional pain and past hurts when not addressed or healed can lead to depression. We feel emotional pain when we fail to achieve, when a loved one dies, or when we are criticized, rejected, or controlled because these types of events involve loss. Disappointment, sadness, grief, fear, anxiety, shame, guilt, and anger can spiral downward and out of control. Mental illness can be a by-product of life. [11]

After scanning the want ads over yet another cup of coffee at the Aristocrat coffee shop on 12th and Granville, Frances was beginning to think about going home. She did like Vancouver, especially on the odd occasion that it was NOT raining and she still desperately sought out adventure. But the bottom line was that she needed a job.

Aside from Frances's desperation, she was beginning to make friends. This was a huge step for her to feel wanted and needed, and most importantly to have a sense of belonging. The other girls from the boarding house were opening up about their own struggles. They shared their love of reading and afternoon matinees, and the dismal lives they had all left behind. Frances brightened when she thought of this. Her new friend Betty was a petite brown eyed brunette who had dragged Frances to a recent USO dance. Frances did not want to go, but boy oh boy, was she ever glad that she did!

United Service Organizations were everywhere during World War ll. Some were run out of established or newly constructed buildings. Others were run out of homes, barns, museums, railroad sleeping cars, and churches. Frances enjoyed meeting soldiers and having many dance partners, conversations, and laughs, which led to coffee dates, dinners, picnics, and afternoon matinees. There was always some fun to be had.

Frances slid off her stool at the counter, folding the want ads up under her arm and grabbing her umbrella from the stand. When she stepped outside a rarity had occurred—the sun was shining! It was splendidly jarring in its brightness and intensity. At that exact moment Frances seemed to stand a little taller. Bright yellow daffodils and blushing red tulips sent a sweet-smelling breeze wafting into the air when Frances began her walk to the boarding house. Pink blossoms exploded and burst from the trees. How remarkable, she thought.

Within minutes the world had changed for Frances. The streets were lined with trees, small little trees with oodles of pink flowers encouraging Frances to touch them. "Is my luck changing" she whispered under her breath? Could this be a sign, she wondered? The years of Catholicism ingrained in her head told Frances not to be superstitious but, much to the horror of the nuns, Frances did believe in luck and good fortune. And she had the feeling that her luck was about to change.

Vancouver Taxis

The original Vancouver train station

Cable car to downtown Vancouver

CHAPTER 4

Gambling and Death

THE TRAIN CHUGGED AND STEAMED ALONG, EMITTING SMOKE and soot as it huffed and puffed towards the mountains, heading west. After the night on top of the box car, Vince woke from a fitful sleep. As daylight approached, Vince was lost in the epic scenery. A towering, majestic backdrop, were these fearsome Rocky Mountains that he had only heard about and never seen. How grand that a poor boy from a small prairie town could experience something so breath-taking. In a dream-like state, Vince found solace in the picture postcard scene that was unfolding before him.

The grandiose beauty was a welcome distraction from the shaking and rattling of the train. Vince felt as though his limbs would come loose from the constant sway and jostle, and from holding on for dear life. With his eyes burning from the putrid stench and his head pounding from lack of food, it was a grateful thought that this train was part of the answer to many questions that plagued Vince's heart.

Earlier on Vince had witnessed an alarming sight. A fight broke out between two drunkards fighting for the same spot on top of the same box car that Vince had come to know as his new home. His safe haven. He had figured out just where to grip, just where to sit, and just where to hold on with his legs and arms to keep stable. In witnessing the rumble, he had thought the bigger fellow would have won, but it was the wiry little guy that seemed to have more stamina; a cagey little man, not much bigger than himself. There was a lot of yelling with fists flying, and Vince felt a familiarity in the cussing. Then, in a split second, the larger man was gone. Vince couldn't say what exactly happened. It was like he was never even there in the first place. The yelling ceased. There was no loud bang or thud to the ground, just immediate silence. It was as if the tall, burly man was wiped off the face of the earth in one fell swoop. Gone, leaving only the empty space where he once was. Vince looked onward, the mountains still standing in all their imposing glory, none the wiser.

Vince felt for his money that was securely pinned inside of his long johns, with his trousers pulled on over top. He felt a sense of fear and foreboding creep into his inner core. Removing his hand from the large safety pin and grabbing a piece of black liquorice, Vince allowed the sweet taste to bring comfort to his recurring, pessimistic thoughts. He looked around, eyeing up the bodies that huddled around him. His Uncle Chuck slept lightly, periodically snoring but still semi-conscious. Some lay on their sides playing cards and others stared blankly into the oncoming night. What were they thinking and where were they going? What brought them to this place? Each one had a story to tell, each one ravaged by poverty and desperation. What ordeal or sorrow had they experienced? It seemed that almost all of them had a bottle of some sort which, to Vince, did not mix well with a life and death situation. Or perhaps it did. He understood the idea of numbing his pain, how the burning, toxic liquid could bring him peace, a release from the constant worry. But then what? Did the hooch take away one's predicament or magnify it, making it worse?

Wise beyond his years, Vince kept to himself. Remembering the advice of his Uncle, "No eye contact" and "Stay close." This seemingly valuable information was soon abolished as the train came to a grinding halt. Leaping up, almost in a panic, Chuck bellowed, "Stay right here. I have some business to take care of." As startled as Vince was, he made no effort to speak or move from his spot that he had quite nicely nestled into. Fatigue came upon him soon after the train stopped. Weary from the continuous movement and jolting about, Vince began to drift into a stress-induced sleep. It felt as if only minutes had passed since Uncle Chuck climbed down the ladder of the train, leaving Vince alone on top of the box car. Actually, it had been hours. Two whole hours to be exact.

Upon waking, Vince found himself alone, immediately feeling a rush of heat to his face and an ache in the pit of his stomach. Looming over Vince was Uncle Chuck, a small slight man who somehow now seemed larger than life. Confused and uncertain, Vince stared blankly up into his uncle's bleary eyes. With his heart racing and his ears ringing Vince knew that Chuck was drunk. Three sheets to the wind, buzzed, wasted, completely tanked. The familiar panic that Vince had become accustomed to gripped him so intensely that the bile began to rise in his throat. With trepidation he managed to blurt out, "What's wrong Uncle Chuck?" At first, he was relieved that his uncle had returned, but then Vince's senses were alert to his worst fear. Apparently, the train was stopped in a place called Yale, British Columbia.

The Fraser River Gold Rush exploded in the spring of 1858, basically putting British Columbia on the map. 30,000 miners, gold-seekers from across Canada, California, and as far away as Europe, clamoured to the west coast of Canada, moving up along the banks of the Fraser River at Yale, and up further north to the Cariboo.

Yale suddenly became a bustling big city, with hotels, restaurants, and stores along the river. Churches and houses were rapidly built on the hill overlooking the river. Yale was the stopping point for steam boats that carried supplies up the Fraser River from Vancouver. The river past Yale was far too fierce for the boats to go any further, so Yale became the hub. The steamboats docked, unloaded cargo, food, supplies, and new get-rich thinkers of the time, seeking their fortune.

In 1871 the Canadian government promised to build a railway connecting the Atlantic Coast with the Pacific Coast. Before construction of the railway in the 1880s, the Gold Rush was wearing thin, and the town of Yale had started to die down. However, Yale later became a very busy place once again as the main supply area for all the work being done on the railway.

Boat traffic to Yale stopped when the building of the railway was completed, therefore Yale once again began to grow smaller. During the chaos and excitement of the Gold Rush, there was excessive gambling, bar room brawls, and unfortunately, many fires were set either by accident or on purpose, causing destruction to the rugged yet remarkable township of Yale. Though the Gold Rush was largely over by 1927, the gold-bearing sandbars of the Fraser were depleted, and the gold miners had long since gone or spread out into the Cariboo, or further yet to the Klondike. [12,13,14,15]

Vince was elated, knowing that they had made it to B.C. But before the relief had a chance to settle in, Uncle Chuck hurriedly explained that there had been a slight misunderstanding during a card game. The train had been delayed due to some mechanical difficulties. To pass the time Chuck had taken on some fellas in an innocent game of five card stud at one of the hotels. The game turned out to be not so innocent, and the fellas turned out to be an angry bunch. Chuck had run out of money and the fella tending the bar strongly suggested that he pay up on the double or else.

In turn, Chuck was now demanding that Vince give him his money—the sixty dollars that Vince had struggled to save. Chuck knew that he had it hidden somewhere, and he was not about to take no for an answer. Vince felt confident that he could win this dispute as he had so much resting on the only money he had to his name; the money that had taken him over three years to accumulate; the money that was going to take him out of the poverty cycle; the money he was counting on to help him start over.

Uncle Chuck swore on his life that he could win the money back two-fold. They would both be better off for it. As Chuck was an old-time swindler himself, he knew that brute force was not going to work with his street-smart nephew. He pleaded with Vince to hand over his money, for pity's sake. He played the humanity card. Having known Vince his whole life, he knew that Vince had compassion and a keen sense of charity. Vince handed the money over to his uncle. Not only did Chuck lose Vince's money in another card game but he also lost the Model T Ford.

As they resumed their positions on top of the box car, neither one speaking to the other, Vince knew that it was only a matter of time, a few more hours until he could get acquainted with his freedom. Unfortunately, Vancouver would no longer be in the cards for Vince and his Uncle Chuck. Having no car to deliver, there would be hell to pay. With no money left, Vince felt in such a bind that the only solution his thirteen-year-old brain could come up with was to part ways with Uncle Chuck.

Vince would be the first to climb down the ladder from their roost on top of the boxcar, leaving Chuck in his own bewilderment. Upon his descent Vince missed the third rung and painfully banged his chin. He teetered there for a moment, eyes watering as blood streamed down his throat, collecting on the collar of his well-worn jacket. Vince dabbed the blood with his threadbare sleeve, depleted, drained, and exhausted. His legs had given out, and climbing down that ladder was the last straw. He needed to sit down, to lay down and rest.

Contemplating his next move, he surveyed the area and scrutinized the landscape. Looking back over his shoulder, he could see the boxcar that had been his home for what felt like an eternity. As the train began to depart, Vince was left still standing on the platform. He heard the familiar hiss of the engine, and breathed in the thick, black smoke for what he thought was the last time.

Looking ahead, green dense forest lay before him. Thick trees. British Columbian woodlands. A smile crept onto Vince's face. He had made it, no worse for the wear. His eyes creased, and his cheeks tightened, as a loud, earth-shattering laugh came out of him. A laugh like none other—his laugh.

Alone, with new found energy, Vince advanced, scrambling down the embankment away from the train, away from the past, away from the only life that he had ever known. Descending further into the depths of the overgrown abundance of trees, Vince feverishly kept moving. He could not stand still. The smell was fresh. If green had a smell it would smell like this. Dirt—flawless, clean and fresh. He filled his lungs like he was lapping up water after a drought. He ran and jumped over logs while dodging branches and exposed roots. There was a natural order to this forest, to this lay of the land. Rows upon rows of trees.

Later on, he would come to know these trees, every species, category, and description. But not now. Now he needed to find food and shelter. He could not carry on for much longer, not like this. His adrenalin would soon wear off, dwindle, and burn out like the old wood stove back home. Having had very little food and water, and suffering from lack of sleep, Vince began to feel foggy and disoriented. The nagging, never-ending fear had returned; fear of riding the rails, fear that he would plummet to his death while on this journey to the province of opportunity. Death often felt near. Now though, he was alive and he was living.

The bright sun had diminished, the timberland grew thicker, and soon it would be nightfall. An unexpected angst wormed its way into Vince's mind. He was alone, not lonely, just alone. He had not given much thought as to what he would do when he got to B.C., and now with no money and no Uncle Chuck, he needed to think, unravelling recent events that had lead him to this. His will to survive was his saving grace right now.

Vince stopped cold in his tracks. He realized that he did need to go back. Not to the destitute, impoverished prairies, but back to the railway and the township of Yale. He needed to be back on the train, but not to Vancouver. He would try his luck in northern British Columbia. He would head in the other direction.

No longer running and jubilantly hopping over twigs, Vince now walked slowly and steadily back the way he had come. Now penniless, the question that circled in his mind was "Who takes money from a kid?" A real low-life, that's who, thought Vince. That money would have enabled Vince to take care of himself in a new town, a better place, where he could hang his hat and carve out a living for himself. Vince remembered the look in his uncle's eyes, dominating him. There was no arguing, no refusing. He had handed over his money with a lump in his throat and a numbness he would never forget.

He vowed that never again would he be duped out of his hard-earned cash. Nor would he ever get caught up in gambling or crooked card games that were lost before they began, a senseless waste of money. The Model T Ford had been discussed and bragged about for months. Now it had gone in the blink of an eye, like the hand of a foolish card game. Three card stud. Aces are wild.

Heading back to Saskatchewan was not an option. But heading north to Quesnel was a possibility. There had been much discussion from others who rode the rails, about Barkerville, Prince Rupert, Prince George, and a place called Burns Lake. He had heard that a fellow by the name of Billy Barker had struck it rich during the second Gold Rush that hit the Cariboo. Even though the gold rush had long since waned and was practically diminished, Vince hoped and dreamed of the possibilities still ahead.

Once back on the platform, Vince decided to research train times and figure out where he could sleep for the night. Smoothing out his dirty, rumpled clothes and adjusting his cap, he thrust out his chest as he approached the ticket taker. Speaking boldly and with confidence, he asked his questions and was informed that there would be a midnight train to Kamloops that would carry on into the Cariboo. He was warned that it was highly illegal to ride the rails, so bowing his head, he thanked the attendant and scurried off.

Still ravenously hungry, Vince decided to mill about, trying to stay out of the way while keeping an eye on the time. He could not lose another opportunity by missing the next train. To take his mind off his hunger, Vince enjoyed watching the people and all the goings on at the train station. He entertained himself by making up stories as to what each person's situation might be. Perhaps a widow with a downcast expression was grieving the loss of a husband, or a couple holding hands was headed for marital bliss. His made-up stories were either gloriously happy, or wretchedly sad. Nevertheless, it passed the time. Not knowing if Uncle Chuck had disembarked from the train when he did, or if he had carried on to Vancouver, Vince was carefully hoping not to bump into him.

Finally, it came time for Vince to secure a spot on top of the train. Much to his dismay, Vince spotted the conductor, the inspector, and the station master all chatting amongst themselves. Their conversation was hushed but had a stern, disgruntled tone. The sight of the men in uniforms, with furrowed brows, rattled Vince's nerves, and just when he was about to dash out of view, he felt a firm grasp on his shirt at the nape of his neck. Cowering, he turned sheepishly and came eye to eye with none other than Uncle Chuck.

He wasn't sure if he should laugh or cry. In Uncle Chuck

fashion, he let go of Vince and said, "Well aren't you a bedraggled sight for sore eyes. Come on boy, I got us a spot in a box car." Vince soon found out that a boxcar would be a warmer, safer, and far more pleasant way to ride the rails.

At each stop, Vince was ready to disembark. But Chuck would insist he stay, exclaiming to Vince that they needed to jump off at just the right time and just the right location. Hours seemed to pass as slow as molasses. The thick night turned into dim morning light, and then like a vicious circle, dusk was beginning to fall again. The pains in Vince's stomach distracted him so much that he did not notice that the train had once again slowed down. He was sitting on the edge of the boxcar with his legs dangling over, trying to focus on his daydreams, when out of nowhere, he felt the presence of someone behind him. Before he could look around, he felt an immense force push him from behind. His body left the confines of the cold metal cavern and flew out of the boxcar door. Rolling safely down the embankment, the last thing Vince saw was his Uncle Chuck's bleary eyes and toothless grin while holding a thumbs up, yelling, "Go get 'em, boy!"

The brisk, chilly night air brought Vince's attention to the task at hand. With only the light of a slivered moon and a million stars to guide his way, Vince fumbled along an unmarked path. Still elevated, Vince's thirteen-year-old naivety probably saved his life that night. Unaware of the elements around him, Vince stumbled upon an old clapboard cabin. Creaking open the door, Vince floundered and fell to the hard dirt floor. Adjusting his eyes to his new surroundings, Vince spotted an ancient, rust-covered single bed in the corner of the small cabin, devoid of a mattress. Vince lay down on the bare springs and immediately drifted off into a deep sleep, filled with images, memories, and fantasies of the bright new road that lay ahead, an untarnished passage filled with hopes and attainable dreams.

A STREAM OF WARM SUNLIGHT FLOODED THROUGH THE CRACKS of the cabin. It was a cabin that was not built to keep the weather out, but to keep a roof over one's head, a small reprieve from a night of wandering the rich, dark forest. Upon waking, Vince instantly doubled up in pain. The emptiness in his stomach needed attention straight away. But how? Where would he find food, substance, anything to fill the gap and take away the gnawing hunger spasms? He drew in his breath and held it as he fixed his gaze on the ceiling. With his belly extended from the influx of air, the pain subsided momentarily.

Vince noticed the warmth of the sun filtering through the spaces in the walls. His ears were attuned to the birds outside and the crackling of insects on the earth. Looking around the abandoned cabin he noticed that the sun had caught on something in the rafters, a bright, gleaming object, illuminated against the worn grey two by fours. Jumping up onto the bed frame Vince reached up to the joist in the crosspiece of the ceiling. Nudging and working it down, Vince realized he had discovered a bloated tin of sardines. In today's standards one would never consider eating anything from an expanded tin can, knowing full well that botulism would have spoiled the contents inside. Vince's stomach spoke louder than his common sense as he pried open the can. Lapping up every last bit of fleshy, smelly fish, drinking in its goodness, Vince's energy and aspirations returned. Opening the cabin door Vince stepped out on a whole new world. The sun was shining as a grand new day awaited him.

WHAT LAY AHEAD WAS THE STRANGEST CONTRAPTION THAT VINCE had ever seen. Later he would discover that he had happened upon an honest to goodness sawmill. Getting a closer look, Vince read with his grade seven education, words in bold print - HELP WANTED, APPLY WITHIN.

Riding the rails

*Vince trying his hand at panning
for gold in the Cariboo*

CHAPTER 5

Family Business

Mental ill-health, insanity, emotional instability.

Frances Elena Farmer (1913-1970) was an American actress and television host. She is perhaps better known for sensationalised accounts of her life, especially her involuntary commitment to a mental hospital. Over the years Frances was committed to several mental institutions where she underwent shock treatments. It was reported that Frances Farmer did not have a good relationship with her Mother. [16]

AFTER ONLY A FEW MONTHS OF JOB SEARCHING, FRANCES LANDED a job at Boeing Aircraft as a stenographer. She could type like a whiz, take dictation at break-neck speed and had mastered short hand by the age of 14. Her grammar was impeccable. She was a very well-versed young lady with stunning handwriting.

That early spring morning, when Frances's mood had lifted, feeling the spring breeze and enjoying the remarkable blossoms on her walk home from the Aristocrat, she had felt elated. The weather was finally cooperating, perhaps a sign, or a reluctant freak of nature, one could not be sure. The rain had subsided, the dreary clouds had lifted, and Frances was once again optimistic that something was about to change. She could feel it in the air. Arriving back at the boarding house, her friend Betty was waiting in an excited dither. Betty had heard that there was an opening in the office where she worked and thought that Frances should give it a shot. That same afternoon, with resume in hand, Frances took the bus to the Sea Island plant of Boeing Aircraft and got the job.

> In 1939 Boeing of Canada, headquartered at Vancouver, B.C., built a huge manufacturing factory on Sea Island beside the middle arm of the Fraser River to build aircraft for the war effort. Sea Island B.C. was well known during WW II for building PBY Catalina Aircraft for off-shore air patrols, and the mid-section of the B-29. [17]

As a young woman during the 1940s in Vancouver, you either worked at the Shipyards on the North Shore, got a job at Boeing Aircraft on Sea Island, or you settled down and got married. Few were shop girls, inevitably waiting for their hand in marriage. With no eligible bachelors to write home about, Frances enjoyed the life of a single career women, as there was always so much to do and a variety of people to do it with.

The War Worker
Author unknown, circa 1940-ish

At seventeen school seems a bore.
When other guys have gone to war.
To sit in class all day is hard,
When you dream of working at the West Coast Ship Yard.
Then even the girls who are studying sewing,
Would sooner be working swing shift at Boeing.
We may not be old enough yet, to go fighting,
But a War Worker's life, can sure be exciting.
The city's sure the place to be,
The West end famed for its room and board.
Not quite like home but what we can afford.
On Granville Street, both night and day.
You'll find War Workers, out to play.
Some go to movies, some roller skate,
Some sit in bars and talk.
While others seem to spend their time,
Standing under Birk's big clock. [18]

Life was fun and fast paced. Frances enjoyed her job and her new best friend Betty. They were like two peas in a pod, giggling buddies and confidants. They always went on double dates together and spent more time talking about the dates beforehand and afterwards than the actual date itself.

One fellow that Frances was seeing regularly started to seem like a good catch. Melvin Monroe was a very kind, gentle Englishman. Standing about 6 feet 2 inches, with red hair and freckles, he had a rather toothy grin and a sideways smile that allowed you to see all the way to the back of his teeth on one side. Frances was seriously thinking of settling down with Melvin. He was in the Navy and in

Vancouver for an extended period. Frances always loved red hair and because she was 5 feet 10 inches tall she also liked tall men as opposed to shorter, balding men. A problem Frances often faced when attending the USO dances was that when she was seated at a table and got asked to dance, many men were horrified when she stood up, and more times than not, she towered over them! Frances often wished that she had been given the gift of being petite and dainty like her friends Ruth and Betty.

But, as luck would have it Melvin, fortunately, was taller than Frances. Therefore, height was no longer an issue. They also had a lot in common, attending dances, going to the show, and playing cards, to name a few. However, the tipping point came one evening after Frances had made a beautiful ham and scalloped potato dinner. Melvin refused to do the dishes, stating that dishes were women's work. Calling it an awkwardly prescient incident, when later describing it to Betty, Frances started to notice certain characteristics about Melvin that made her skin crawl. Firstly, he had a sniffing problem, sucking mucus back up his nostrils rather than using a hanky to blow it out. It was obnoxious and brought Melvin's likable qualities considerably down in the books. That, and his pompous refusal to help in the kitchen. Frances was relieved when Melvin got called back to his ship and she covertly slipped a Dear John letter into his duffle bag. Que Sera-Sera, whatever will be, will be. Doris Day sang ever so sweetly what Frances was thinking and feeling when she gave ole Melvin the boot!

Aside from the fun and camaraderie with the guys and gals, Frances had a rude awakening when she returned to the boarding house from work one afternoon. Sitting on the front entranceway table was a letter from home, written in her father's perfect penmanship.

Dearest Billy,

Please expect us this Saturday on the 12:00 noon train from Lethbridge. Your mother and I have purchased two homes side by side in a place called Kitsilano. One home for you and your sister Violet and the other home for your mother and myself.

Warmest regards,

Father

In 1940 a gallon of milk cost 34 cents, eggs 45 cents a dozen, a movie ticket was 24 cents, and a house was approximately $6,550.00. The average annual salary was $1,900.00 and minimum wage was 30 cents per hour.

Picking her family up at the train station required two taxi cabs. The first taxi was for the abundance of luggage and the second taxi carried Frances, her sister Violet, her mother Edith, and her father Joe to their new homes in Kitsilano at 5th and Bayswater.

The family chose to move out west in late spring, which was an excellent choice, Frances thought. When she herself moved out in early spring, the Vancouver rain almost got the better of her. It was only this past spring that Frances started to enjoy herself. And now the apple cart was upset yet again, with her entire family underfoot. How on earth would they all manage? Before Frances could give it much more thought, the whirlwind of setting up two homes had begun with an industrious over load.

Edith was an avid shopper. If there was a bargain to be had, Edith would find it. She was also a deep, dark, secretive loner, often at home, brooding and pouting most of the time. The term pouting was used because Edith had a habit of extending her lower lip and sucking her thumb, embarrassing to the family but rarely seen by the public. It was during these instances that Edith made notes and scribbled down random thoughts on little pieces of paper, later to be crumpled up and thrown away by Edith herself. They were scraps containing erratic words and sentences that were incomprehensible to anyone but Edith. They filled and lined the waste paper baskets, indicating that Edith was having a dreadful day.

When not lying low, Edith would once again be flying off the deep end, spending money to her heart's content only to be crippled a few days later with a shroud of despair that no one dared to address. One was never sure what they would wake up to on any given day with Edith. It was subconsciously decided to leave Edith to her own devices on her down days, and to enjoy the fun and her energetic, erratic behaviour on her up days.

Violet too, was an avid shopper, but unlike her mother, she had a horrible temper. When not spending money, Violet would be ranting about something; mad about the carpets taking too long to be delivered, upset because her favourite potato chips were not in stock, and always disagreeing with Frances every chance she got. What made matters worse was Violet's drinking. Her childhood Coca Cola addiction was still in full force, but with age came the legal aspect of a cocktail or two, anytime of day or night. Violet's morning coffee or afternoon tea was often spiked with something of a harder nature, and an afternoon beer or before dinner drink was normal when Violet was around. The fridge and liquor cabinet was always fully stocked.

As for Frances, she was not a shopper or a drinker. In fact, the more Violet drank the more Frances despised it. Together, Joe and Frances would stay out of the way. They would play cribbage at the kitchen table and on the sly, roll their eyes in unison at the carrying on around them.

Every morning when Frances headed to work, Violet and Edith would sleep well into the day, and Joe would set up his carpentry in the downstairs storage room. Having left the CP Rail prior to moving, Joe made himself useful by making furniture for the two side-by-side, ornate Queen Ann-style homes. Not new homes by any means, but built during the turn of the century, each was spacious with matching gingerbread, turrets, and wraparound porches. Many called them Victorians or sometimes "Painted Ladies". Joe and Edith's dwelling was powdered in pastel pinks and seafoam greens while Frances and Violet's manor was astoundingly different, painted a deep burgundy with royal blue trim. Wisteria gallantly wound its way up the spindles on one and the other's front porches. Together the houses were sturdy likenesses, each with single paned windows that shook violently every time Violet slammed the front door. Joe had received an exceptional deal on these older, unpopular character homes that in today's market would be highly valued and not so reasonably priced. Each cost $4500.00 in 1943.

ASIDE FROM THE UPHEAVALS AND EMOTIONAL DISTURBANCES inside the two homes, everything on the outside was moving along quite splendidly. Violet met a sailor (or so he said) and got married within only a week or two of meeting him. Tommy was drop dead gorgeous—tall, dark, and handsome and seemingly a good catch. He could handle Violet and her angry outbursts by speaking sweetly and softly in hushed tones, which at the beginning of their union was just what the doctor had ordered. He had an amazing way with words and could keep up with Violet's drinking sprees quite nicely. Tommy was not a teetotaller, but rather a whiskey sour man.

President Franklin D. Roosevelt announced the Repeal of Prohibition on December 5, 1933, ending the unpopular nationwide prohibition of alcohol. On a social level, many people felt that alcohol contributed to crime, domestic violence, and the growth of "saloon" culture. However, it had two major unintended consequences. Prohibition caused people to want to drink more, reducing people's respect for the law. Going to places like speakeasies became glamorous and exciting. People developed a more cavalier attitude towards breaking the laws in general. Organized crime, in turn, flourished, since making and transporting and selling alcohol was illegal, so it was up to criminals to meet this demand. Since demand was so high, the criminal gangs became rich. In these ways, Prohibition had profound consequences that helped make North America in some ways a more lawless place. [19]

Tommy had made his fortune during these times smuggling whiskey, spirits, and whatever was being touted across the border to Canada at the time. Tommy was somewhat of an outlaw and incredibly desirable to Violet. Ten years after the ending of Prohibition, Tommy was still living off the wealth that he had incurred during his criminal phase, giving Tommy and Violet disposable income and lots of time to bicker, drink, and carry on. Tommy was anything but a Sailor!

Frances, on the other hand, was about to meet the love of her life. While on a double blind date, sweet demure Frances found herself holding hands under the table with Betty's blind date. He was a charming, handsome stranger who would soon steal Frances's heart and change her life forever.

*Stepping out
on the town*

The house at 5th and Bayswater

The Aristocrat on Granville Street, Vancouver BC

Fun at the beach

CHAPTER 6

Finding Them

WHEN UNCLE CHUCK AND VINCE PARTED WAYS AFTER THE GAM-bling incident, Chuck handed Vince a crumpled-up piece of paper with some contact names, people who could help him possibly find lodging, work, and even safety. Not giving the shredded, worn paper much thought, Vince shoved it into his pants pocket and proceeded to forget about it. Finding shelter and food was enough for a thirteen-year-old boy to handle, 3,000 miles away from home. After bedding down in the old dilapidated shack that Vince had stumbled upon, the day began with hope on the horizon. That morning, noticing the Help Wanted sign, Vince looked around nervously and tried to find someone within this deep wooded area for help. Catching him off-guard, the sudden whir of activity required a moment for Vince to gain courage and momentum.

Taking in his surroundings, Vince noticed a half dozen able-bodied men furiously working. Machines were buzzing, trees larger than life were rolling, and voices were all speaking at once. Finally, Vince settled on a slender man with stooped shoulders and kind eyes to approach first. "Excuse me Mister. I noticed the Help Wanted sign, and I'm looking for a job," Vince said, all 100 lbs. of him, with his shoulders back, chest out and chin jutting forward.

Vince continued on, "I'm a good worker, I'll do as I'm told, and I won't cause you any trouble."

Vince chose the right man that day. Any of the other strapping young men would have told him to "scram, take a hike kid," but not this kind hearted, sympathetic stranger. You see, this man had seven children of his own. He had hungry mouths to feed, a house to keep fuelled and warm, and a baby on the way, all in amongst the Great Depression. Not only did this man find pity on Vince and give him a job on that chilly October morning, but he also shared his meagre lunch, and invited Vince home at the end of the twelve-hour work day.

Vince's first job was to learn about every part of the sawmill and how each one worked and was used. It was dangerous work. By watching the Head Sawyer, who was operating the controls of the Saw Carriage, Vince learned quickly. Years later, although he was ashamed of only having a Grade Seven education, he always noticed and wondered why he had more common sense and street smarts than any University Scholar he had ever met. Vince was never told, but knew in his heart of hearts, that he was brilliant at certain things. Some things just came easy to Vince. Delving into learning and impressing his new boss, Vince quickly grasped how to operate a circular saw and a band saw.

THE HEAD SAWYER LOOKED FOR THE MOST VALUABLE LUMBER, the highest grade, and it was his responsibility to avoid defects in the log being cut. Next was the Resaw Operator, similar to the Head Sawyer, whose job was to make the first cut boards perfectly square. This took a keen eye and tremendous patience. Because Vince was small, he was quickly trained at removing the wane or rounded bark edges from the boards as they came from the head saw. Later on, Vince would be trained as a Lumber Grader. This job was less back breaking and was usually designated for the older men. Because of his lack of upper body strength and being a small teenager, they used Vince for his perfect vision, to grade the lumber. The lumber had to be examined as it passed through on a conveyor belt, looking for such defects as splits, knots, faulty edges, stains, and unsatisfactory machine work. These workers had to keep a tally of specified grades and board footage required to fill an order. Thus, math skills were needed and quickly developed. Unbeknownst to Vince, his manipulation of numbers was very keen.

Chain Off bearers physically pulled lumber from a moving conveyor. They would slide and stack lumber in piles, sorting them according to the lumber grade marked on each piece of lumber. This took strength that Vince had not yet acquired, and was a job saved for the stocky, stronger men.

Lumber Handling Equipment Operators, also known as Carrier Drivers, operated the machinery that grasped the logs to move them to the logging trucks. Millwrights were a separate department altogether, but nevertheless over time, Vince was to learn this position as well. Millwrights routinely inspected the machines to keep the conveyors, dryers, and other wood processing equipment adjusted and in working order. This all took time and months of learning—on the job training, so to speak. Vince was a shoe-in for promotion after promotion.

GOING BACK TO VINCE'S FIRST DAY OF REAL WORK, NOT ONLY WAS it mind boggling and frightening, it was also uplifting and freeing. Vince would come to make 25 cents a week. More importantly, Vince would come to know a family, being fed and clothed and loved. For the man who hired Vince on his first morning in B.C. was the same man whose name was scrawled on the rumpled, rolled up piece of paper in Vince's pocket that Chuck had thrust into the palm of his hand on that last day before Vince fled from the boxcar.

Settling into an exuberant new family and a completely new lifestyle, Vince soon grew into a man.

Physical hard labour, home cooked food, and most importantly, companionship, were three aspects of life that Vince had not yet tapped into. Soon after arriving in Burns Lake, he willingly and even-handedly learned everything there was to learn about trees, lumber, and sawmills. Combining a concrete job with good nutrition, Vince developed into a handsome, responsible, hardworking young man.

Working at the mill, as busy as he was, it was not difficult for Vince to block out the past. Only at night in the dark corners of his mind did the years of abuse come flooding back to him. Waking in a cold sweat on numerous occasions, startled at his surroundings, Vince developed an aversion to sleep. Arising at 3 or 4 in the morning happy to begin his day, thankful for the distraction that morning brought, he slipped quietly from the confines of his bed. In the grey early morning dawn, wanting to earn his keep with his new family, Vince collected wood and kindling to heat the wood stove. Sometimes he forced his thoughts to make sense of his family history that felt like a million years ago. Here alone, in the early morning before the others arose, Vince would unwind the past like an old, worn rug. He would tug and pull at the threads of memory to unravel the tightly woven pain, and the thoughts that weighed him down at moments like this, by himself, with no witnesses to the tears of heartbreak that would stream down his face.

Carrying in kindling and bundles from the wood shed, Vince concluded on this one winter morning that his name must have been the cause, the root for the endless teasing. Vincent Alphonse Bonner. Where in god's name did his parents come up with a name such as that, he wondered, having never been told and having no one to ask. "Innocent Vinnocent," the children would sing, taunting and cracking up with laughter. "Hey, Alphonse, you're as big as an elephant. Your name should be Alaphants," they'd continue to chime in. Vince would run. That is all he could think of to do.

Run and run and run, until the voices trailed off, becoming faint. Once he was clear and well enough away from the bullies, the tears would begin to flow. His muffled cries were all he had. "Why won't they leave me alone?" he thought as he gasped for air between each sob. These flashbacks were fixtures in his mind, difficult not to dwell on during these god-forsaken mornings. Seldom would Vince be free of the continuous tirade of voices from his past. He would wonder when it would stop hurting.

As the bright sun began to heat up the below-freezing morning air, Vince knew that his life was taking a turn for the better. The Burns family was seeing to that. Each morning while he readied himself for the day, there was validation. Mrs. Burns marvelled at Vince's capabilities. How wonderful to have this young man dutifully pitching in wherever there was a need. On this Saturday morning, work at the mill had become sparse due to heavy snow fall. So, while some leisurely slept in, others were up with the crows. Vince had the fire built by 4:00 a.m. so the farm house was toasty warm, quite a treat to wake up to on this minus 15 morning. Fresh, kind-hearted faces began meandering through and about the small kitchen. Vince willingly and exuberantly greeted his adopted family, grateful to get out of his head the vicious circle of thoughts that feverishly consumed him.

Frying eggs and bacon in the old cast iron frying pan, Vince threw in the day old, homemade bread, watching it sizzle and sear in the bacon grease until the corners turned up crisp and golden brown. As he pondered the day ahead while sweating over the heat of the cook stove, Vince's thoughts were taken to the vision of Mary, a sweet little brunette that he had seen around town of late. At eighteen, Vince was ready to settle down, to start a family of his own. Maybe then he would be free from his past, free to make memories of his own with a genuine family to raise and nurture. The town hall dance was tonight, he would ask Mary to waltz and perhaps he'd be able to tell if his affections for her were mutual!

As Vince became familiar with the logging industry, he came to know of other options for keeping employed during slow times at the mill. Occasionally, he would find work in one of the logging camps with the rough-and-tumble lumberjacks. A lumberjack is a worker in the logging industry who performs the initial harvesting and transport of trees for processing into forest products. The term originated in the early 1900s and because of its historical ties, it became part of British Columbia's folklore. The actual work was difficult, dangerous, seasonal, low-paying, and living conditions in the logging camps were not pleasant. However, the men built a culture that was based on strength, masculinity, confrontation with danger, and resistance to modernization. Lumberjacks were exclusively men. The camps were bunkhouses or tents, and the common equipment they used included an axe and a cross-cut saw.

Logger Sports grew out of competition in lumber camps to see who the best lumberjack was. It also filled in the spaces of time when they were not working. If machines were down or the weather did not permit a typical day of work, the men would clamour to an afternoon of logger sports fun. It created camaraderie among the men and it helped ward off loneliness, isolation from loved ones, and the boredom of down time.

Perhaps from not playing sports as a child, and the fact that Vince was painfully shy, he did not have a competitive bone in his body. However, he was extremely strong, agile, and coordinated, and he knew how to amuse himself and those around him. As he came into his own, eventually forcing his shyness aside, it gave him great pleasure to make people laugh. Having a story or joke somewhere up his sleeve became Vince's new image.

From the mid-1930s onward, during Vince's time in the logging camps, his claim to fame was log rolling, a sport that involved two competitors, each on one end of a free-floating log in a body of water. The lumberjacks battled to stay on the log by sprinting, kicking the log, and using a variety of techniques as they attempted to cause their opponent to fall off. Matches usually consisted of three out of five falls. The winner would stand on top of the wet rolling log and the loser would end up in the freezing cold water. Vince rarely lost at this event, mostly for fear of the water as he was never taught to swim, and had only self-taught skills that would barely save his life if it was necessary.

The skills that Vince learned in the logging camps would benefit him much later in life, ensuring his capability with anything involving trees. He came to know every type of tree and what its wood was best used for. Timber, power saws, tools of any kind, and sawmills were all familiar to him.

Vince also became a leading tree faller. Falling trees is the process of downing individual trees. The person cutting the tree is known as a Faller. "Fallers" did the actual job of felling a tree with axes and saws. Once felled and delimbed, a tree was either cut into logs by a "bucker" or skidded or hauled to a railroad or river for transportation.

In addition to logging, the men had to take turns at other duties in and around the logging camp. Some were more reluctant than others to pitch in whenever help was needed. Vince was always eager to please and keep busy, often volunteering as the camp cook if they happened to be without one.

With limited food supplies, the men frequently complained about their meals, and the lack of quantity and quality. The items missed the most were desserts, sweet treats to balance out the meal and offer something to look forward to at the end of an exhausting, physically taxing day.

Several times, Vince's imagination had to work overtime when it came to creating delicious, nutritious, and filling meals. Foodstuffs and replenishments came inconsistently every few weeks, and sometimes not at all. Aged potatoes, greying meat, cooking oats, and an occasional shipment of stale bread were to be expected.

A few staples such as salt, powdered milk, coffee, and sometimes sugar concluded the provisions. On the other hand, every once in a while there was an unexpected gem nestled in among the usual fare; a surprise that one did not necessarily recognize or know what to do with.

On a dreary day in early spring, Banana Extract was what Vince came upon after unpacking one of the shipments. Being the fun-loving story teller that Vince was, over breakfast one morning, Vince promised the men that a tasty, satisfying dessert would be accompanying their meal that night. After shouts and hoots of disbelief, the men looked at Vince in bewilderment, and something as simple as the promise of a treat that evening made the entire camp buzz with excitement. For the entire day men were having bets as to what the sweet concoction could possibly be.

Vince spent the better part of the day peeling, cooking, and mashing potatoes. He added dry powdered milk, minimal rations of sugar, and Banana Extract! Whipping and beating until his arm was numb, and stiff, light peaks formed out of the creamy mass, and by the end of the day his delectable masterpiece was completed.

Following the usual bland meal that night, using every pot and kettle, Vince brought in a bounty of decadent Banana Pudding for the curious diners. Upon seeing the dessert, his fellow loggers almost became delirious with joy, smacking Vince on the back, jumping up on the wooden benches and pounding their fists on the tables in unison, laughing and praising Vince Bonner for their reward. Known just as Bonner, he became the star of the camp that night. Every man ate Vince's Banana pudding until their sides were splitting. Not a soul knew that they had just consumed a simple batch of mashed potatoes, with a few imaginative ingredients added on the sly.

General information sources referred to for this chapter. [20, 21]

Logging way back when, Northern BC

Good humoured Vince,

enjoying a beer after a hard day

Burns Lake British Columbia, from rail

A typical small-town sawmill

CHAPTER 7

A First and Last Love

WHY ARE WE FASCINATED WITH KNOWING THE FUTURE AND WHAT lies ahead? Tomorrow, the next day, months from now; business ventures, travel plans, investments; real estate endeavours, relationships, and planning, planning, planning.

Back in 1945, if Frances could have seen what was in the cards for her, she may have chosen a different path. She might have spoken up more, pushed through barriers, and climbed over obstacles. For some reason life has a way of just happening. We all have hopes and dreams, desires and aspirations. But as the phrase goes, "shit happens."

After one chance meeting, Frances fell deeply and madly in love, as did Vince. It just so happened to be with each other.

Frances had no intention of falling in love. In fact she had no desire to even be going on a double date with Betty that night. The drab rainy months of November had turned into the colder rainy months of December and a date was not the first thing on Frances's mind. What she really wanted to do was to curl up with an enjoyable book and forget about everything.

THINGS WITH HER FAMILY WERE NOT GOING WELL. VIOLET AND
Tommy were always fighting, and her mother would lock herself
in her room in the house next door for days on end. Frances
still played cards regularly with her dad and occasionally went to
wrestling matches. Her dad loved wrestling and Frances still had
her tom boy image to live up to. Rumour has it that at one of the
matches she became so involved that she went up and tapped the
opponent with her umbrella! When she realised what she had done,
she hastily went to sit down, embarrassed at her impulsiveness! She
was now twenty-four years old and did not know what her future
held. The clock was ticking. She thought about Ruth back at home
in Taber and their dreams of becoming private investigators.
The thought of her childhood friend always brought a smile to
Frances's face.

ON THE VERY SAME DECEMBER MORNING, VINCE WAS DOWN FROM
up north, visiting Vancouver for a break, to collect his thoughts and
re-group. He had learned pretty much everything there was to learn
about logging and sawmills up in northern British Columbia. And
not surprising, Vince had even gotten married. Perhaps sounding
blunt, and for lack of a better word, his marriage had failed.

After proposing to Mary, the cute little brunette in Burns Lake,
they married, and moved to Quenelle, British Columbia. Vince
worked long hours in a logging camp, while his new bride stayed
home in their little log cabin. It was a short marriage—perhaps they
were both too young and immature. Both seeking love, neither
having learned from example what a good marriage should or could
be like, or how to achieve it. The marriage eventually ended in
divorce after Vince found Mary in the arms of another man when
he came home from work earlier than usual one day.

Frances Gervais and Betty Carmichael were being picked up
that night by Ernie Swanson and Vince Bonner—a blind date. Two

best friends, on a double date with two best friends. They were to spend the evening at the Cave Supper Club.

OPENING IN 1937 TO 1981 AT 626 HORNBY STREET IN DOWNTOWN Vancouver, the Cave Supper Club was the place to be. Performers from all over North America came to entertain. Couples flocked to dance the night away to the likes of Louis Armstrong, Oscar Peterson, Lenny Bruce, Duke Ellington, Stan Getz, Fats Domino, Ray Charles, Johnny Cash, Jim Reeves, Sonny and Cher, Lena Horne, Wayne Newton, Diana Ross, Everly Brothers, Roy Orbison, Buddy Rich and many more.

It was on this rainy cold December night that fate would have its way. Frances had been paired up with Ernie, and Betty had been paired up with Vince. Ernie was the comical, gangly type, while Vince was suave and debonair. In spite of this pairing, Frances and Vince felt an immediate attraction towards one another. And even though they had each arrived with another, they secretly held hands under the dinner table between dances. Thus began their courtship.

Fran & Vince, their first date

Outside the Cave, street view, Vancouver

Inside of the Cave dance hall, Vancouver

CHAPTER 8

Who Takes This Woman?

FRANCES AND VINCE, MY MOTHER AND FATHER, WERE MARRIED on a brisk sunny day, December 15th, 1946, by a Justice of the Peace at the Vancouver Courthouse. Frances, at twenty-five years, was considered old, border-line spinster material back in the day, and Vince was thirty with a previous failed marriage under his belt.

Frances wore a navy-blue skirt with matching suit jacket, a navy pill box hat covered in baby's breath for a subtle veil. Beige pumps and navy gloves tied the whole outfit together. Standing five feet ten inches at 120 lbs Frances had never looked prettier. Often told that she was too thin and too tall, she always considered herself to be plain, but her beauty was simple and feminine. No fuss and no muss. Her fine blonde hair resembled corn silk, and her pale blue eyes had captured Vince's heart from the moment he first laid eyes on her only sixteen months earlier.

Vince wore a basic black suit and tie with a crisp, white collared shirt. He always had impeccable posture but he stood even taller than usual that day next to Frances, his new bride to be. Shoulders back, chest bursting with pride, and grinning from ear to ear, Vince's olive skin, black wavy hair, and green eyes enhanced his boyish good looks. He was a man and ready to be the best husband he could possibly be.

Only one photo remains to mark their nuptials because shortly after they said "I do," the photo studio burned to the ground, leaving behind only one photograph of the happy couple. Because of Frances's earlier Catholic beliefs she was not superstitious. Therefore, the lack of photos—the tragic loss, would never be considered an omen of what was to come.

All they wanted was a small, intimate ceremony with no guests or frills. Money was tight, and Frances and Vince were saving to purchase a lot and build their own home. The plan was to live with Violet and Tommy until they had saved the $4500.00 they needed for the land and the estimated cost of building their dream home in North Vancouver. It was a far cry from Vince's meagre beginnings in Saskatchewan, riding the rails to BC and settling in Burns Lake. In his mind, each part of his journey was bringing him closer to meeting and marrying Frances and further away from the past he had long since tried to bury and forget, often without success.

WORLD WAR II HAD RECENTLY ENDED AND CANADA WAS IN A STATE of grieving the lost. 40,000 men served the U-boats but 30,000 never returned. Canada's troops were also made up of black and aboriginal peoples. After the war ended, Canada agreed to accept displaced people and refugees from Europe. For these reasons Canada in turn experienced a baby boom and there was much celebration and hopefulness on the horizon. Post-War Canada had a more tolerant society, a bigger population, a booming economy, more power, and a better government. Frances and Vince felt that it was the perfect time to get married.

In Frances's mind, she was not getting any younger, wondering how many more comments from her mother she could endure about being an old maid, and Vince desperately longed for the family that he never had.

Standing before the Judge, Vince's mind once again began to wander. Weddings are a time of family and friends, but not today. Frances and Vince would stand alone, each having one attendant, their best friends. Betty was standing up for Frances and Ernie for Vince. How Vince wished that their nuptials could be different, a huge country wedding with an abundance of family and close friends, a nice storybook kick off. Neither Frances's nor Vince's parents would be in attendance when they tied the knot on this day.

VINCE HAD HEARD THAT HIS FATHER EARL AND YOUNGER WIFE Esther had relocated to Kelowna to a small hobby farm, and it was nine years ago, almost to the day, that Vince had searched out and found his own mother, the women who had abandoned him in the small prairie shack, so many years before.

Unbeknownst to Vince, his mother had greatly wanted to see him again too. Not a day had gone by where she did not think about him. She had gone on to marry another abusive man, having more children, and regretting that she had not brought Vince and his brother Hank with her when she fled with Vince's sisters. She had always hoped that her two sons made it out alive, but never knew their eventual fate.

Vince had tracked down his mother by spending copious lonely nights in the logging camps, writing letters to as many relatives as he could think of. He waited hopefully for word on his mother and two sisters Bonnie and Geneva, whom he had not heard from since he was five years old. All this time, through the comfortless days of physical hard labour and writing letters in the evening, Vince's grade seven grammar and penmanship dramatically improved. During a fit of loneliness while at one of the work camps, with no letters written back to him, Vince decided to mail himself a beautifully gift-wrapped tie, mainly for all his efforts in writing letters out and having nothing to show for it in the way of responses and letters back. Like the other men in the camp, he too wanted something to open on mail day. How he would fuss over the splendid gift that had arrived in the mail just for him, never telling a soul until years later, that he had mailed himself a gift to make it appear that he had a family or friends that cared about him.

Eventually Vince had an address to contact his mother in North Dakota, and word came back that she was happy and excited to meet up with him. She had no means with little money and a brood of children that still needed looking after. So after the mill had shut down for the winter, Vince climbed aboard the train that would take him across the prairies and down to the state of North Dakota, in the United States of America, to finally reconnect with his mother.

As Vince disembarked from the train on that memorable cold winter day, he stood for a moment, not sure if he would recognize or even know his mother. Standing on the platform, waving and beaming, his mother Martha knew her son instantly. Even though it had been sixteen years since they had last been together, a mother has a never ceasing bond, instincts, and immeasurable love regarding her children. One could say a mother never forgets. With tears streaming down her face, upon seeing Vince in a sea of strangers, she called out his nick name. "Vino, Vino, over here!" she exclaimed. Vince clamoured from the stoop and ran to his mother's embrace. She was bigger and stronger than he had remembered and with that, she picked twenty-one-year-old Vince up off the ground and hugged him with a force he had never felt before. Vince had finally been reunited with his past; his mother, the first woman who had broken his heart. However, time heals most wounds, and on this fateful day neither he nor his mother felt any anger for the lost years, only joy from their new-found connection.

Vince was also delighted to reconnect with his sisters. He was astounded at their beauty— magnificent jet-black hair, soft curls, and olive skin, just like his own. They spent more than a week getting to know one another and promised to not let too much time pass before they would see each other again. Catching up, telling stories and sharing the same sense of humour is exactly what families do, Vince thought. Saying goodbye to his mother, sisters, and half siblings was bitter sweet. Vince knew in his heart that he had a family, and even if it was a torn, broken family, he at least had one.

As Vince now repeated his vows to Frances before their friends and the judge, a lump stuck in his throat, and his voice was lost somewhere between the emotions of missing his mother, and elation at marrying a remarkable woman that he was sure he had dreamed up, an intelligent, beautiful woman who loved him back just the same. They would have a future together, a family, a home, and a life.

Everything leading up to this momentous occasion now seemed like a blur, a whirlwind romance. After their initial meeting on the blind date back at the Cave Night Club, Vince had headed back up north for work. They wrote letters back and forth and they both had high hopes for a bright future together. Frances continued at Boeing, coming home in the evenings to unexpected drama. Violet spent most of her days drinking and stewing with jealousy over Tommy's guilt or innocence on any given topic. Frances was sure to get an earful from Violet every night after returning from work. In addition to the incessant banter was the likelihood of running into rearranged furniture or brand-new appliances, purchases made on a whim by Violet, depending on her moods, as they could swing one way or another as quickly as the revolving door at the Hudson's Bay Company.

Frances had become weary of her sister's antics, her father's denial, and her mother's pouting and thumb sucking. She just wanted a life of her own. She found herself often recollecting when she had once said goodbye to her family and best friend Ruth, only five short years ago on the train platform back in Taber. And now here they were, together again. Nothing had changed except their location.

Vince, on the other hand, was desperate to get back to Frances. After being away for nine months, fed up, Vince walked into the Foreman's office at the logging camp and handed in his resignation. Within twenty four hours, and nine months after saying goodbye to Frances, Vince was back in Vancouver. With four handwritten love letters from Frances, her home address, and high hopes that they could be a couple, Vince set out to find his one true love. Walking up and down the streets of Kitsilano he finally found the two houses, side by side, where Violet, Tommy, Frances, and her parents lived. Knocking on the door, which was answered by a striking blonde, Vince asked if there was a Frances at home. Little did he know that it was Frances who had answered the door and with that, she slammed the door in Vince's face, most perturbed that he did not recognize her.

Ringing the bell again, Vince stammered his apology and explained how her beauty and his nerves had thrown him off. They later had a good laugh about it and their courting began, with their eventual wedding only 7 months later. The honeymoon was at the Vancouver Hotel and then the weekend was spent in Seattle.

KNOWN FOR HIS SENSE OF HUMOUR, ERNIE SWANSON GOT SO drunk at the wedding that he ended up handcuffing himself to the taxi cab that was to take Frances and Vince to their hotel. It was meant to be a practical joke but seemingly was not quite so funny to the newlyweds. Eventually the police and a locksmith were called, and Ernie was set free with a few handshakes and pats on the back. Early the next morning, Frances and Vince boarded the train that would whisk them away to Seattle, Washington, a glamorous city in the U.S. only three hours from downtown Vancouver.

Returning from Seattle, Frances and Vince settled in quite nicely with Tommy and Violet, living rent free next door to parents Joe and Edith. Everyone seemed to manoeuvre around each other quite smoothly. Edith adored Vince. She waited on him hand and foot. Since the wedding, a dark cloud had lifted from Edith and she was like a spring chicken clucking all about in an excited chitter chatter towards Vince, school girlish and flirty. This bothered no one and the entire family was quite relieved because Edith in a slump was no fun for anyone. Joe took everything in stride and was also relieved that Edith had emerged from the doldrums, cooking and cleaning, busying herself with baking and waiting for Vince to return from work.

Vince had easily found a job for a small excavating company, clearing land for subdivisions in and around the Vancouver area, basically working 9 – 5 with weekends off. After years of working seven days a week, this was a welcome change, as it gave Vince time to enjoy his new life, with his wife and a built-in extended family. Frances and Vince would spend their weekends taking day trips to White Rock Beach, having picnics at Lost Lagoon, and playing cards in the evenings. They both loved the movie theatre and would think nothing of sitting through three picture shows in a row at the Stanley Theatre on Granville Street. Edith was at home preparing elaborate lunches that were always waiting for them upon their return. All of Vince's favourite foods would be set before them: pickled herrings, devilled eggs, and sardines on toast. Afterwards there was always dessert of chocolate cake or various pies such as lemon or apple.

After months of wedded bliss for Frances and Vince, Tommy and Violet became comfortable enough to show their true colours. They began to openly fight like cats and dogs, regardless of who was in earshot. Both unemployed and living off Tommy's dwindling savings, they were irritable and discontent on most days. The nights were filled with clinking ice cubes in glasses of rum, smoke filled rooms, and slurred conversation over games of cards. Rarely would a game be finished before the card table was overturned or Violet was throwing a drink in Tommy's face.

On numerous occasions Vince would come home from an eight-hour day of pushing topsoil to find a locked front door with Violet on the other side sweetly trying to coax Tommy inside, Tommy having fled to the nearest cable car, nowhere to be seen. Vince would be alone, standing on the front porch trying to see where the elusive Tommy was. As he worked the door knob he would be startled and horrified to find himself in a choke hold of Violet's wrath. On one occasion, coming home from work, Vince opened the door to find Violet waiting on the other side with a butcher knife (intended for Tommy) that was thrust at Vince, barely missing his face. With all the strength he could muster, Vince managed to wrestle Violet to the floor and with all his might he removed the knife from Violet's deranged grasp. Inevitably this was the beginning of the end for the two couples sharing accommodation.

*Vince & Hank reuniting
with their mother*

Vince & Frances
tying the knot

*Vince's pretty
sister Bonnie*

Frances, Edith, Tommy, Violet

CHAPTER 9

Breakfast at 5th and Bayswater

AS A HUSBAND, VINCE WAS FUN, COMICAL, AND ALWAYS A BARREL of laughs. Frances loved to laugh and could find humour in the oddities of life. They were a well-matched couple, compatible and busy with entertaining activities and events. Both were optimistic, hopeful, and living for the moment while planning their future.

By 1946 standards, Frances wore the pants in the family. Due to Vince's easy-going nature he freely handed his pay checks and social calendar over to Frances. Vince worked at a bulldozing company driving Cats, and did odd jobs around both houses. Frances still worked at Boeing, took care of the bills, groceries, insurance, taxes, and social outings.

Growing up without a mother, Vince enjoyed and relished in a female's approach. He highly regarded Frances's brains and beauty as a complete package and thanked his lucky stars every day when leaving for work as he kissed Frances goodbye. Every night when he laid down beside her, he drifted off into a well-deserved peaceful sleep, no longer plagued with the nightmares from his past.

Vince began to feel as though his first marriage did not count in the grand scheme of things, but was more of a mistake, or rather a practice run in finding true love. Initially heartbroken but divorcing amicably, neither Vince nor his first wife Mary had any regrets, hard feelings, or remorse. They were young and inexperienced at life. After the incident with Mary's affair, they decided to go their separate ways. Therefore, a smooth transition was made into his marriage to Frances. It was wedded bliss until death do they part.

Frances, having never been a morning person, began Vince's tradition of bringing her breakfast in bed. Everyday just before dawn, Vince would make his way to their modern kitchen in their 5th and Bayswater, Kitsilano, Victorian style home. He would put the kettle on to make instant coffee, and then make dry toast with a skiff of strawberry jam (no butter) for Frances. Without a word he would deliver the light fare, leaving it at her bedside table.

Vince often shared his mornings before work with Edith, who had also fallen madly in love with Frances's new husband as a devoted mother in-law. Never having been an early riser herself, Edith treasured her mornings with Vince. Her new son in-law gave her a purpose for getting out of bed. Vince was animated, friendly, and kind. Edith thought that Vince did not know her history of mood swings and dark days where she would hide away to brood, never thinking that Frances had shared a few deep secrets of her own, one of them being her relationship with her mother. Vince never let on to Edith all that he knew.

It had become Edith's mission to send Vince out the door for work with a hearty lunch consisting of roast beef sandwiches on thick white homemade bread, smothered in horse radish and Keen's mustard, and a thick slab of chocolate cake or raisin pie for dessert. Vince never failed to lavish Edith with praise, animated conversation, and a wealth of compliments. Edith had never been happier. As Vince said goodbye for the day and made his way up to the West Broadway street car, Edith was left wondering how her plain, tom boy daughter Frances had landed such a remarkable man.

When Frances did not have her nose in a book, she was delighted to be out and about in the city with Vince. They had a revolving list of activities that kept them busy and entertained. In the spring and summer, they would take the cable car to Granville and Burrard and hop on a bus to Stanley Park.

They would make their way past the rose garden to Lost Lagoon for a canoe paddle and a box lunch, taking time to smell the bright yellow roses and aromatic lilac trees along the way. Vince made a mental note to plant both at some point in his lifetime to remember these initial stages of their marriage. While Vince rowed and manoeuvred the canoe, Frances looked on, enjoying the cherry blossom trees lining the edge of the water, flowering puffs of pink candy bursting from gnarly branches. Weeping willow trees bowed down in admiration to the couple, as their canoe glided past. Cucumber and ham sandwiches, shortbread cookies, and a Coke, made for a perfect picnic and a perfect date. The cost was twenty-five cents, not cheap with Vince's wage of one dollar a day as a Cat operator. Frances was earning seven dollars per week still working at Boeing and was able to put every pay check into their joint savings account.

Stanley Park, 1,001 acres, was opened to the public on September 27, 1988. It was named after Lord Stanley of Preston, 16th Earl of Derby, a British politician and Canada's governor-general at the time.

The land was originally used by indigenous peoples for thousands of years before British Columbia was colonized. For many years after the 1858 Fraser Canyon Gold Rush and colonisation, the future park was also home to non-aboriginal settlers. The land was later turned into Vancouver's first park when the city incorporated in 1886.

The park is almost surrounded by water, with approximately half a million trees, some of which stand up to 249 feet and are up to hundreds of years old. Thousands of trees were lost over the past 100 years due to extreme wind storms, but many were replaced.

Most of the man-made structures were built between 1911 and 1937. Additional attractions such as the (now not used) Polar Bear exhibit, current aquarium and miniature train, were added in the post-war period. Significant effort was put into building the near 100-year-old seawall that runs around the perimeter of the park. Forests, trails, beaches, lakes, fish & chips stands, Malkin Bowl and children's play areas is what makes Stanley Park a favourite place to local residents and tourists alike.

The Stanley Park Rose Garden was established in 1920 by the Kiwanis Club, a service organisation. The garden contains over 3,500 rose bushes in the summer. But there are many other colourful flowers to be seen in the spring and fall as well.

Lost Lagoon was named by poet E. Pauline Johnson, for when the tide was in, water lapped the shores of the West End of Vancouver. When the water retreated with the tide, the lagoon disappeared entirely. The mud flats were a source for clams for the Squamish nation that lived in the area, and its name was Ch'ekxwa'7lech, meaning "gets dry at times".

Lost Lagoon is situated on the edge of the city at the entrance of Stanley Park. Between 1916 and 1926 the Stanley Park Causeway was built, land locking the water entirely. In 1922 the Vancouver Park Board officially called it "Lost Lagoon". The next phase came in 1929, when the salt water pipes entering from Coal Harbour were shut off, turning the lagoon into a fresh water lake. The BC Fish and Game Protection Association was given permission to stock the lake with trout. The Stanley formed, and people were charged to fish there. This came to an end in 1938 when a walkway around the lake was constructed and the area declared a bird sanctuary. The row boats remained and canoes were brought for rentals. [22]

Lost Lagoon
By Emily Pauline Johnson

It is dusk on the Lost Lagoon,
And we two dreaming the dusk away,
Beneath the drift of a twilight grey,
Beneath the drowse of an ending day,
And the curve of a golden moon.

It is dark in the Lost Lagoon,
And gone are the depths of haunting blue,
The grouping gulls, and the old canoe,
The singing firs, and the dusk and-you,
And gone is the golden moon.

O! Lure of the Lost Lagoon, --
I dream tonight that my paddle blurs
The purple shade where seaweed stirs,
I hear the call of the singing firs
In the hush of the golden moon.

Emily Pauline Johnson (also known in the Mohawk as Tekahionwake) was a Canadian writer and performer in the late 19th century. Johnson was notable for her poems and performances that celebrated her Aboriginal heritage; her father was a Mohawk chief of mixed ancestry. Her mother was an English immigrant.

Johnson's poetry was published in Canada and the United States and she was vocal in establishing Canadian Literature. While her literary reputation declined after her death, a complete collection of her work was published in 2002. She was born March 10, 1885 and died March 7, 1913 at the age 51. Her resting place is Stanley Park, Vancouver, British Columbia. [23]

In addition to their many outings, it was a rare occasion to attend a theatre performance at the Malkin Bowl theatre at Stanley Park. A sheer delight for Frances, while Vince on the other hand, was not fond of dramatic performances or musicals, as his realistic approach to life would not bring about a song and dance in the middle of a rain storm, but rather a strategy to keep dry and find something to do indoors. Frances loved the *Theatre under the Stars*, so this was on their to-do list in the summer months in the mid 1940's. Frances followed the entertainment section of the Vancouver Sun to keep up with all the performances.

> The Marion Malkin Memorial Bowl is an outdoor theatre in Stanley Park. Built in 1934, it was meant to be a two-thirds-size replica of the Hollywood Bowl in Los Angeles. Allard de Ridder, then conductor of the Vancouver Symphony Orchestra, was responsible for persuading W.H. Malkin, a former mayor of Vancouver, to build the theatre as a summer concert venue for the VSO. Malkin endowed the theatre in memory of his wife, Marion.
>
> Malkin Bowl is home to 'Theatre under the Stars,' or TUTS. Before that it was home to the Vancouver Civic Theatre Society, founded in 1940, officially opening on August 6, 1940, with "A Midsummer Night's Dream" being one of the many first performances. "As You Like It," "The Belle of New York," "Anything Goes," "Bitter Sweet," "The Chocolate Soldier," "The Desert Song," and "Blossom Time" were hits from 1940 to 1949. [24]

In the first few years of their marriage, the weekends would be spent in deep conversation, as they were still getting to know one another. Vince would share small snippets of his tumultuous childhood which led to a discussion, collectively, about what their future hopes and dreams were. Periodically during their time together, silence was often welcomed by Frances, but not always a priority as Vince had a knack for filling in the spaces!

Raised a Catholic with an uncommunicative mother, Catholic nuns at school, and Church and Mass on Sundays, Frances grew into womanhood with guilt, shame, and naivety. In retrospect, Frances often summed up her childhood as being filled with hypocrisy on the outside while living a fairy tale life on the inside, rebellious to her mother's wishes while indulging herself in reading novels of fiction filled with adventure, mystery, and espionage.

Frances thought that she was dying, that death was beckoning her on that dreadful morning when she encountered her first period, that time of month that young girls are either prepared for or devastated by. It was not a blessing, but a curse. The birds and the bees, anatomy, and God forbid, puberty was never a topic of conversation. Later, when it came time to consummate her marriage, Frances was not ready and in no rush.

Vince, forever the gentleman, perceived Frances's reluctance to become intimate not as a problem or worry at all. Thrilled to have a wife, friend, and lifelong companion, Vince knew that they both wanted children, so in this situation, patience would be a virtue.

A year into their marriage, eventually the time was right, the deed was done and just like magic Frances became pregnant, a pregnancy without incident. Gaining sixty pounds, Frances coasted along eating well and giving up smoking, only because it felt like the right thing to do. In the 1940s the surgeon general had not discovered the health risks of smoking, in fact most doctors would smoke right along with their patients. Delivering babies, giving examinations in a smoke-filled, nicotine infused labour room, or doctor's office was considered normal. With reports on the hazards of smoking not emerging until the 1970s, Frances was ahead of her time only because not smoking felt like the right thing to do.

Nine months later a beautiful baby girl was born. Edith rejoiced, Vince beamed with pride, Violet seethed with envy, Joe stood on the side-lines, and Frances looked on. As duty called for wife and mother, Frances did not know anything about babies, so she was happy to let Vince change the diapers and allowed Edith to participate in all the feedings. Frances loved her baby as much as she loved the escape of reading. Together mother and daughter would sit quietly with opinions and views flying over their heads—Violet and Tommy fighting more than ever and Vince chattering away with jokes and stories to keep the house mates and family members entertained.

Upon choosing a name for their daughter, Vince was adamant to pick a name that could not be made fun of. Terribly taunted and teased as a child, he could not stand for his own flesh and blood to have the same treatment. Just the smallest thought of his childhood brought back a tightness in his gut that could be stirred up as if it were yesterday.

After much deliberation, together Frances and Vince came up with the name Linda Dawn Bonner, a fine name. Not only was it a popular name in 1947, but it was also pretty and seemingly void of words that could be rhymed to cause an outpouring of mean insults from other children.

It wasn't until grade one that Linda came home crying from the first day of school, exclaiming that the other children in her class had called her Linda Pinda! Immediately realising that children could be mean for assorted reasons, Frances's advice was for Linda to go back to school the next day and sock her assailants in the eye. This did not sit well with Linda, with the two of them eventually becoming opposite in every way.

With the obvious wedded bliss of Frances and Vince, plus the arrival of their new baby, Violet could not contain her jealousy.

She was no longer dazzled by Tommy's good looks or charmed by his gangster persona. Violet was repulsed by Tommy's inability to get a job, bored with their constant bickering, and unimpressed with his constant drinking. The romance was over, and Violet wanted out. She wanted what Frances had, a deep meaningful relationship to a handsome, successful man.

Long before Violet made the decision to leave, Tommy had confided in Vince that the marriage was over. Tommy complained about how mean and unpredictable Violet was and admitted that he was afraid of her, sleeping with one eye open and his shoes at the side of the bed for an easy getaway. Vince had to agree with Tommy that Violet's behaviour had gotten worse, and together they planned Tommy's escape.

Unbeknownst to anyone, Violet had already taken up with a helicopter pilot by the name of Elliot. He was a rich American business tycoon who was trying to establish a hunting and fishing lodge in Northern B.C. They met at the Sears and Roebuck department store when they were both trying to purchase some fishing tackle in the sporting goods department. Violet was also an outdoors woman, which enamoured Elliot. She could do almost anything she set her mind to, but had never worked a day in her life. Nor did she like to read and could drink any man under the table. She played poker with the best of them and smoked cigars like they were going out of style. Violet could have been a powerful, successful woman had it not been for everything being handed to her on a silver platter. Plus, her addiction to alcohol and the same mood swings that debilitated her mother made day to day life exhausting for everyone, even Violet herself.

Tommy left in the middle of the night when he felt the coast was clear, Violet not noticing he had left until three days later. Coming in from another day of gallivanting around town with Elliot, Violet observed that some items were missing. Tommy's shoes at the door, his toiletries from the bathroom cupboard, and eventually when she looked a little closer, most of his clothes from their shared closet were gone. For dramatic effect, Tommy left behind his gold wedding band, next to his whiskey glass on the night stand. Initially shocked and then with a shrug of her shoulders and a shot of whiskey, Violet started to get ready for her next date with Elliot.

Good riddance, Edith thought. Joe and Frances said nothing, and Vince was saddened. He liked Tommy, and Vince knew that he would miss Tommy's far-fetched stories from his prohibition days. Even though Tommy was a tame drunk, causing no harm to anyone, Vince knew in his heart that something had to change, before Tommy and Violet killed each other. Or Tommy ended up dead.

After Tommy left, Violet globe-trotted from Vancouver to Seattle with Elliot, up north for fishing and hunting, and down to Reno, Nevada for gambling. Eventually she settled with Elliot in a small town called Vernon, British Columbia. Violet loved the dry, scorching summers and the cool, crisp winters completely free of rain. The Okanagan was a lot like her home town of Taber, Alberta.

EVENTUALLY, VIOLET WOULD ACQUIRE NOT ONE, BUT THREE Pinky's Laundromats in Vernon. These were easily recognized by the Pink Elephant Logo, which was a cute circular sign with an elephant's curved trunk tooting out the word 'Pinky's.' The coin-operated washers and dryers were also pink and the rest of the décor was pastel yellow. Violet became somewhat of a celebrity as the owner of these laundromats.

On either side of her first Pinky's was a coffee shop and a hair salon. This proved to be convenient for Violet, as she would often sit in the coffee shop before opening her business, drinking her coffee and smoking. At the end of day she had a standing appointment at the beauty parlour to get her hair set. Then it was off to the Legion to drink and dance the night away. Over time, she hired staff for the business and then spent most of the days collecting the money and visiting in the local coffee shops, with various people from the town. Everyone knew who Violet was and they all wanted to stay on her good side, because one never knew daily what state of mind she would be in or how quickly her mood could turn from light to dark.

FRANCES AND VINCE DECIDED THAT IT WAS TIME TO ALSO VENTURE out on their own. With Linda being three years old, they wanted to be settled in their own home before she started school and in advance of another child, a sibling for Linda, a son for Vince, and a grandson for Grandpa Joe.

Soon the building would begin on a lot they had acquired in North Vancouver.

In 1865 the first sawmill was purchased by Sewell Prescott Moody to become an area of North Vancouver known as Moodyville, with a hotel and the first school on the North Shore. Eventually becoming the oldest surviving church in the lower mainland, St. Paul's Church was erected where Squamish families were settling. The first electric lights came to Moodyville in 1892. By 1900 a passenger ferry began running from the foot of Lonsdale to Downtown Vancouver. In 1904 a car ferry was added, and the service continued until 1958. Led by Chief Joe Capilano in 1908, talks with Prime Minister Wilfred Laurier about land claims, fishing and hunting rights, and education were the topics of discussion.

When Alfred St. George Hamersley bought land to the west of Moodyville and began selling lots, Lower Lonsdale then became the heart of the community. Things were booming, progress was being made. By 1925 with the growth of the ship yards, a mill at Indian Arm, a few dry good shops, a mercantile, ferries, cable cars and the first grain terminal, North Vancouver became the hub for starting out as a family. [25]

In 1952, Frances, Vince, and Linda moved into their newly built home on East 18th and Moody Avenue, in the city of North Vancouver. Their next child Douglas was born in 1953, and he was to take the place of everyone's sweetheart, big sister Linda. Douglas had deep brown eyes and olive skin like his father, but his face held a more serious expression than Vince's. His sombre character only made him more endearing.

In 1956 came an unexpected pregnancy and the arrival of Kenneth, marking his debut as the blue-eyed blonde that would steal his mother's heart. Resembling Frances much more than the other two, Kenneth would grow up to be charming and jovial. Finally, in 1960 at the age of 39, Frances delivered her last baby. A surprise, an accident, not in the cards, but welcomed just the same. Frances wanted the name of her last daughter to be Brook, but Vince was keen on the name Karen. Frances agreed and added on the middle name Ruth, after her long time best friend. She found out years later that Ruth named her youngest daughter after Frances; Connie Frances and Karen Ruth. The girls eventually met and hit it off just like their mothers did before them.

Karen would soon become the apple of her father's eye and his shadow, following him everywhere he went.

Due to the last two pregnancies being unplanned, Vince decided to take care of matters so a fifth child did not join their humble abode unexpectedly. While Frances was recuperating he took it upon himself to get a vasectomy. They were illegal still in Canada, but one could travel across the border to Bellingham and for a few days' pay, some family planning and birth prevention could take place. This was not a customary practice in the 1960s but after word got out, Vince was driving men down across the line in car loads to get the procedure done. The neighbourhood wives were thrilled and Vince became known as the Vasectomy Chauffeur of North Vancouver!

Edith and Joe remained in the Kitsilano 5th and Bayswater home for another five years. After the two couples left, they sold one of the houses, doubling their profit, as the city was growing at breakneck speed. With the Depression era a distant memory and the end of World War ll, people had an elated sense of renewal. Houses were selling fast.

With her two daughters no longer living next door, and her entertaining son in-law no longer giving purpose to waking up in the morning, Edith was feeling a sense of loss. Her depression came with the tides and the only glimmer of hope was when her granddaughter Linda would travel over on the bus from North Vancouver to see her. They would bake while Linda talked about her day and how she loved her baby brother Douglas. She would chatter non-stop, a little like her father, which gave Edith comfort. Eventually, Linda climbed back aboard the bus, all by herself, to travel over two bridges and home to North Vancouver.

Edith missed Violet terribly. Two peas in a pod they were, and yet together they became oil and water, mother and daughter, yin and yang. When word came that Elliot had died in a helicopter crash, Violet became distraught and comatose. Edith immediately raced to be with her eldest daughter.

The remedy for Violet's grief was prescription Valium. Also known as Diazepam, it was originally used to treat anxiety, sleep disorders, and alcohol withdrawal. Better to bury the pain than to let it rise to the surface, bubble over, and be dealt with, or so it was thought by Violet and her Doctor. Over time the Valium would numb the pain but, when combined with Violet's alcohol consumption, her psychotic behaviour increased.

Intermittent Explosive Disorder, Borderline Personality Disorder, Antisocial Personality Disorder, all similar in nature but completely unheard of until the early 1970s. Behavioural disorders characterized by explosive outbursts of anger and violence, often to the point of rage, such as impulsive screaming, impulsive aggression; not premeditated. Prior to the outbursts, one feels an immediate mood change, energy changes and tension. Often associated with bipolar disorder, the aggressive acts can be accompanied by a sensation of relief and in some cases pleasure, followed later by remorse, impairment of functioning, or financial and legal consequences.

In the early 19th century people afflicted with psychological disorders were placed in workhouses, madhouses, or asylums because it was too burdensome for the families to care for them.

By 1963 there had been much reform, and mental health issues were beginning to get more respect, with the attitude of a softer, gentler approach implemented. The introduction of pharmacology led to the deinstitutionalisation reform which changed the view to "community-oriented care' to improve the "quality of life".

However, the stigma of mental illness has only just more recently been improved with awareness, funding and a mental health balance that is taught and implemented more freely.
26, 27, 28

Rather than place Violet into a sanatorium, Edith arrived by Greyhound bus from Vancouver to be at Violet's side as a care giver, a shoulder to lean on, and a mother to offer wisdom, all completely foreign duties to Edith.

Unfortunately, Violet's problems were bigger than both of them. Grieving the loss of Elliot, addicted to alcohol and prescription drugs, Violet had started hallucinating. She had gone deeply into debt, borrowing money from loan sharks to survive. The bank was just about to seize her mobile home when Edith arrived with her check book in hand. Bailing Violet out financially was only the tip of the iceberg. With Edith's own mental illness, she was not equipped or experienced at assisting someone else who was in worse shape than herself. Violet had always frightened her right down to her inner core, but Edith was entranced by Violet's manipulation and lies.

One night, shortly after Edith's arrival, Violet woke up not long after they had bedded down, screaming bloody murder. She literally thought that Edith was trying to murder her while she lay sleeping. With the commotion, Edith was woken from her own fitful sleep to find Violet looming over her bed. Scrambling to get out of the way of Violet's wrath, Edith ran outside into the trailer park, with Violet close behind.

Both women were clothed in full length night gowns and the full moon lent eerie illumination to the tangled flurry. Mother and daughter, wild-eyed and frightened, stumbled through the neighbourhood in a game of cat and mouse. Eventually, neighbours began to emerge. Regardless of their feelings for Violet, she was yet again disturbing the peace, and something needed to be done. The police were called, arriving to Edith's pleas begging for them to stay out of it. Pushing past Edith, the police apprehended Violet, placing her in a strait jacket and whisking her away. Edith was left behind, staring in horror and bewilderment at the disappearing taillights of the Paddy Wagon.

Going back inside the trailer, Edith freshened up and, perfectly coiffed, called a taxi to take her to the hospital. Violet remained in the psychiatric ward for six weeks. Her medication was altered, and she had time to dry out. Edith visited the hospital daily, bringing homemade soups and biscuits, the latest movie magazines, and gifts of jewellery and various trinkets to hopefully bring Violet out of her slump.

When all was said and done, Violet detoxed and was sent back to her mobile home trailer park where the two women managed until they could send for Joe. Watching soap operas, reading the newspaper, cleaning, and cooking lavish meals, they barely emerged from the trailer. Seven years would pass and, in the meantime, Joe would live with Frances, Vince, and their four children, biding his time, enjoying his grandchildren, attending his Catholic church, writing letters to Edith, and reading diligently from his Bible.

City Bus and streetcar meet, North Vancouver

Tommy, Joe, Vince at Stanley Park

And baby
makes three,
newborn Linda

Frances, Vince,
Edith

Violet and
Elliot, her
new boyfriend

Edith shopping
on Granville Street,
Vancouver

*Stanley Park
in the earlier day
Vancouver*

*Skating on
Lost Lagoon,
Vancouver*

*Malkin Bowl –
Theater Under
the Stars, Vancouver*

CHAPTER 10

Dance with a Dolly

Dance with a Dolly

By Tony Pastor

As I was walkin' down the street, down the street, down the street

I met somebody who was mighty sweet, mighty fair to see

I asked her would she like to have a talk, have a talk, make some talk

All the fellows standin' on the walk, wishin' they were me.

Mama, Mama let me dress up tonight, dress up tonight, dress up tonight,

I've got a secret, gonna 'fess up tonight

Gonna dance by the light of the moon.

Gonna dance with a dolly with a hole in her stockin'

While our knees keep aknockin' and our toes keep arockin'

Dance with a dolly with a hole in her stockin'

Dance by the light of the moon.

Mama, Mama put the cat out tonight,

Cat out tonight, cat out tonight

Worked all day I'm gonna scat out tonight

And I won't be home until dawn.

Gonna dance with the dolly with a hole in her stockin'
While our knees keep a knockin' and our toes keep a rockin '
Dance with a dolly with a hole in her stockin'
Dance by the light of the moon
Gonna dance by the light of the moon. [29]

MY FATHER COULD SING AND CARRY A TUNE; HE COULD DANCE
and belt out tunes like a famous entertainer. As my father told it,
growing up in a small town during the Depression Era with little
to do, the kids and grownups would make their own fun—singing
contests, dancing contests, endless games of charades and skits
from the very young to the unquestionably old. He also had stories
to tell me, heart wrenchingly sad stories of real events from his
childhood and youth, and sometimes funny and adventurous
anecdotes that had me spell bound. Like the time when a circus
came to town and one of the lions had escaped. Not knowing this,
my father was walking home late one night from a local dance.
As he made his way through a marsh he suddenly came face to
face with two bright yellow, circular eyeballs, about chest level to
himself. When he felt a hot, moist wind of breath on his neck and
face, all he could think to do was run like hell. It was only later, on
the next morning that he figured out it was the escaped lion from
the circus which he had encountered in the dead of night while
walking home through the marsh. His stories were vivid and full
of expression that captured my heart and my mind.

A favourite treat for me was when my father would place my
feet upon his and dance me around the house, while he belted out
the song, *Dance with a Dolly*. I still know the words to this day, even
if they did not make a lot of sense then or now.

In 1962 there was no such thing as a leash law. In other words, dogs roamed freely to and fro, wandering around neighbourhoods, pooping anywhere they wanted and chasing cats to their hearts' content. It was on a warm summer morning when my mother became hysterical for the first time in her life. As she was hanging out the clothes on this bright June morning she froze in her laundry duties when out of the bird- chirping sky came blood curdling screams. She knew instantly that it was her child, her youngest daughter—me.

At two years old I too could wander freely, but mostly in my own unfenced back yard. On this occasion the neighbour's dog Kirk, a retired German Shepherd police dog, had come meandering into our back yard to take a nap. Noticing that he had fallen asleep on my toy drum, I bent over to tug it out from underneath the massive hound. With my actions spooking the dog, he snapped his head around and dug his giant teeth into my two-year-old little head.

Another neighbour had been out in his garage toying away at his car when he heard the commotion. Looking up, he ran to my aid and wrapped my head in an old dirty rag. Picking me up, he met my mother half way up our walkway. He then drove bloody and bleeding Karen and hysterical Frances to the emergency department at Lions Gate Hospital.

The wound required thirty-four stitches from the nape of my neck up the back of my skull to the top of my forehead. The doctors and nurses were able to pick out bits of gravel from my face, stitch me back together, wrap my head in a turban-style bandage and send us home. I could only be propped up on a couch to sit quietly.

There was no way to reach my father during and after the traumatic event as he was out and about at various construction sites. At 5:00 p.m. when he returned home from work, my mother met him at the door to fill him in on the days' goings on. He proceeded to sit with me, promising to end the dog's life with his bare hands if necessary. On hearing this I cried and said, "No daddy, please don't hurt the doggy!" I still like dogs to this day, and yet I have always been flattered to hear my father tell the tales of how he tried to do away with Kirk, the meanest dog on the planet.

The neighbourhood all banded together with a petition to have Kirk put to sleep, because he had frightened others before me. However, in 1962 the law was that a dog was allowed two bites, and/or two dog attacks before he could be put down. Kirk lived on, eventually dying of old age.

MARIO WAS MY FIRST FRIEND. HE LIVED NEXT DOOR IN A TINY green house surrounded by an immense forest. He had two older brothers and a baby sister. His mother made the best spaghetti known to man, woman, or child! Never had I ever tasted anything as delicious as Anne Hocevar's spaghetti! Mario and I called on one another on a regular basis for a few years before I started school. After that we rarely saw each other.

As best buddies, we freely roamed the neighbourhood, tootling around pretending and playing and never checking in at home unless we were hungry or had to go to the bathroom. The secret boulder on the corner of our block was a favourite go-to meeting place for Mario and me. We sat side by side and took turns driving the immense boulder as a pretend car or bulldozer. We would often enjoy a picnic lunch of peanut butter and jam sandwiches while we played. My mother always gave us a choice of folded over bread or a cut in half sandwich. Folded over was the usual preference as the white bread was soft and fluffy and made for a nice gigantic bite from the center, allowing sugary jam and sticky peanut butter to ooze down one's arm or get stuck on our little ruddy faces until bedtime.

EVERY MORNING, EVEN AFTER I HAD LONG SINCE MOVED AWAY, my father would bring my mother her breakfast in bed. He was a morning person, my mother was not. He would kiss my mother every morning on the lips before he left for work in his coveralls, clean and ready for a day of dirt and diesel oil, tending to his bulldozing business. After rising, my mother would put on her usual attire for the day, a floral house dress with a zipper up the front and big pockets to hold clothes pegs and wadded up Kleenex.

I could be guaranteed an enormous bear hug and kiss on the cheek daily from my dad. I would regularly ask my father if I was pretty and he would always respond with "Yes!" and follow up by tickling and tousling me around like a rag doll, promising to bring me something home after work, a treat, a toy, a special rock—some memorable keepsake that he had stumbled upon in his daily travels.

On occasion if I was lucky, my father would take me to work with him. My three older siblings would all be at school and I would get to go with my daddy, travelling around to different job sites and places he needed to be. Climbing up into his black and white Ford International pickup truck was a stretch but with wiry little arms, I managed. The name "Vince Bonner's Bulldozing" was emblazoned in red on both front doors, his business logo and North Vancouver claim to fame. He always preferred Fords. Off we would go, listening to the Country and Western radio station, headed to work.

Out on the road with my dad, everywhere we went we were greeted with smiles, handshakes and laughter; jokes that I did not fully understand but I would laugh along with just the same. Everyone called me "Smiley", the nick-name that I was known by to all my dad's cohorts and business associates. "Here comes Smiley, Vince Bonner's little foreman," would be exclaimed by many.

There were regular stops, one being the corner store, long before 7-11 and Macs Milk graced the corners. Leaving me waiting in the truck, my father would go into the family-run store, returning with a box of Cracker Jacks that depicted a little sailor boy on the side saluting whomever was dumb enough to purchase the dried up little kernels of sugared popcorn. The best part was the dinky prize at the bottom of the box. These were an assortment of junk, glorious tiny baubles ranging from a build-your-own plastic car, a miniature magnifying glass, and sometimes a blue sapphire ring that was adjustable for every finger. Little bits of caramelized corn combined with stale peanuts had to be dug through before reaching the prize below. I adored my father and could never bring myself to tell him that I despised the favourite thing that he liked to buy me. So, unknown to him, I would carefully drop the hardened pellets of corn one at a time out the window of the truck while he was driving. I enjoyed my prize at the bottom and nibbled on just one or two pieces of popcorn for good measure.

Finning Tractor was a drive across town. We had a different route than the one my mother took when we went to the movies. Instead of taking the Lions Gate Bridge, dad would go over The Second Narrows Bridge. I would always request the story of how the bridge fell down while it was being built. My father would recall the historical, tragic day, always paying homage to the brave men who climbed the girders, risking and sometimes losing their lives. Included in the telling of the tragic event was how the sound of the bridge coming down could be heard all over North Vancouver.

On June 17, 1958 two spans of the Second Narrows Bridge, then under construction, collapsed into Burrard Inlet, killing 19 men in what remains the worst industrial disaster in Vancouver's history. The period of construction was February 1956 – August 25, 1960 (official opening). The bridge now has the official name of Iron Workers Memorial Second Narrows Crossing.

The collapse occurred near quitting time at about 3:40 p.m. Ironworkers suspended 40 meters above the water heard a horrific noise as one of the spans began to crash into the inlet in a mass of tangled steel. The momentum dislocated the columns, causing another span to tumble into the ocean. 79 workers fell. Among the dead were 14 ironworkers, 3 engineers, a painter, and a commercial diver who died a few days later when he drowned trying to recover a body. 20 others were seriously injured. The design for the temporary span supports was done by engineer John McKibbin, who made several errors that were not caught by the engineer in charge, Murray McDonald. The historian of the bridge disaster, Eric Jamieson, has noted that McKibbin's role in the collapse was only one factor – others included questionable steel quality and lax engineering practices. McKibbin was killed in the collapse. [30]

Once over the bridge our route included driving past the PNE, or Pacific National Exhibition, officially opened in 1910 by then Canadian Prime Minister Sir Wilfrid Laurier. The fair was a showcase of British Columbia to the rest of Canada and the world, and was the second largest event of its kind in North America, behind the New York State Fair. During its seventeen-day duration, people would travel from all over Canada and parts of the US to attend. In particular, the residents of Vancouver and the Lower Mainland made attending the PNE a traditional event. In every final report card at the end of the school year would be two free tickets for the fair. This was a huge highlight. Before one would check if they had passed their grade, they would first check to find their PNE tickets to the fair. These in turn brought on excitement and anticipation for a fun-filled day at the fair. Held every year near the end of the summer, one would chronicle their endless summer days knowing that they still had the fair to look forward to before the end of a blissful summer and before shopping for school supplies.

The biggest draws at the PNE were the assortment of farm animals, the midway of games and rides, and the ever so popular food pavilion. The adults had venues too, and many knives, slicers, dicers, and mixers were purchased to prove it. Just driving past the PNE even if it was not fair time, I couldn't help but recall the pink and blue, sickening sweet fluffs of cotton candy, the red candy apples that stuck in my teeth, the helium balloons I let go of to watch sail aimlessly to the heavens, the rides, and the stuffed animals my father would undoubtedly win for me. After a twelve-hour day at the fair, I would fall into bed at night, completely exhausted.

Driving for another ten minutes, we would eventually pull up to Finning Tractor, both of us scrambling out of the truck, with me traipsing after my dad trying to catch up to hold his hand as we entered the big sliding doors. We were acknowledged by the very pretty receptionist as she buzzed the parts department. All of my dad's bulldozers were from Finning's. Various parts were sometimes required, and conversations followed about how things were going with these enormous excavators. Everyone knew him by name and he was again greeted with smiles and handshakes. In fact, the red carpet was always rolled out for us wherever we went. I beamed with pride knowing that my dad was the best, and almost certain that my dad must be famous.

When finished at Finning's, it was back to the North Shore and over to the job site to deliver the part we had just picked up. My father would proudly climb up onto the Cat's seat, hoisting me up to sit beside him. As he drove and manoeuvred the Cat, I was there to see first-hand his handy work, smelling the rich top soil and hearing the engine roar, bringing comfort and a sense of trust to little four-year-old me. There was never a thought or a worry about ear protection, seat belts, or fluorescent vests. Even though hardhats and steel-toed boots were a must, nothing much was said about Smiley, the little foreman sitting up beside her hero.

HEADING HOME FOR LUNCH AS MY DAD DID EVERY DAY, WE ANTIC-ipated a steaming bowl of Campbell's tomato soup with smashed up crackers or tuna fish sandwiches and sometimes grilled cheese or sardines on toast. My dad loved sardines on toast. Lunch would be waiting for us. Afterwards I would play with my dolls, draw, colour, or play outside on the swing my father had built high up between two aging cedar trees. The entire neighbourhood of children frequently lived in our yard. Swinging, playing in the playhouse, or my brother's favourite games of Cowboys and Indians or Cops and Robbers. At that time of the afternoon with the big kids all at school, I would settle on my dearest and most cherished friend, my doll Marky. Marky was a monkey the size of a two-year-old child. My Auntie Bonnie had given him to me. Sometimes my two brothers would hang Marky up from his suspenders and treat him like a punching bag, until my howls of complaints would cease their antics, and all would be good again.

My Auntie Bonnie was my favourite aunt. She was my dad's youngest sister who lived in America. Auntie Bonnie was beautiful and funny. When she visited us, her make-up kit filled an entire suitcase. It snapped open and had trays and mirrors and was filled to the brim with cosmetics. My mother only wore red lipstick and rouge. Auntie Bonnie's array of make-up, lotions and potions was extremely impressive. Looking back I now admire my mother's simplicity, but in the 60's my Auntie Bonnie's charisma, fancy clothes, and jet black wavy hair was everything to me. When family and friends commented on how much I resembled her, I felt beautiful and pleased with myself. How must my mother have felt? Never once showing signs of jealousy or envy, my mother's school of thought was, "If they love my children, they love me." She considered herself to be plain and too tall. My father on the other hand had tanned skin from working outdoors, strong callused hands, and a bright white smile always plastered on his face. His loud, boisterous laugh could be heard all the way down the block to our neighbours' homes. It was only later that I figured out he had many tears when no one was around.

The Tears of a Clown
By Smokey Robinson

Chorus:
Now there are some sad things known to man
But ain't too much sadder than
The tears of a clown when there's no one around,
Just like Pagliacci did
I try to keep my surface hid
Smiling in the crowd I try
But in my lonely room I cry
The tears of a clown
When there's no one around
Now if there's a smile on my face
Don't let my glad expression
Give you the wrong impression
Don't let this smile I wear
Make you think that I don't care
'Cause really I'm sad. [31]

Perhaps the details of my father's childhood had been shared to my mother many years prior; how he had grown up without sisters or a mother, and how he rode the rails to find freedom—freedom from rejection, poverty, and abuse. When all attention was lavished on my father, his sense of humour, and exuberant story-telling, the gentle nature my mother displayed was a lesson to all of us. There were never any raised voices, yelling, or arguing in our home. My father told me numerous times that he vowed a long time ago that his children would not see or hear an angry word or tone of voice. He never allowed teasing as siblings often do. If sibling rivalry did occur, I would see a darkness come over my father's persona. He would become quiet and often leave the room, allowing (or leaving) my mother to straighten things out, reprimand or send the culprit to their room.

Laughter was comfortable and easy for my dad, but not angry emotions.

THESE CARE-FREE DAYS OF SPENDING TIME WITH MY FRIENDS AND my father, would soon give way to red Kool-Aid and graham wafers, a tiny kitchen with baby dolls in toy strollers, a plastic mat on the floor for napping, and my mother waiting for me at the door—when middle class children were four years old in 1964 they went to kindergarten. It was a new concept. It was a kick-start to the wheel of education, a preamble to the treadmill of being in an institution for the next twelve years; front end loading us for what was to come. Some enjoyed their two and half hours in the basement of a church, where others, such as myself, were terrified. When you are the youngest of four children what do you do when they all leave for school? Who looks after you? Where do you go? How do you fill your time?

Studies have shown that if one has no memory of a certain time in their life, they may have blocked it out, due to trauma; buried it deep within; erased it from their mind as if thinking about it was far too painful to recollect.

I have no memory of Grade One. Looking at myself and class mates in the end-of-year school photo, empty six-year-old faces stare back at me, expressions blank and devoid of emotion. Where did Smiley go? Little hands folded in her lap, eyes as round as saucers and a tight lipped, pouty face that could break your heart. That was me.

The year was 1966. No more trips in the pickup truck to work with Daddy or lazy days playing with Marky and Mario. No more helping my Mom bake chocolate chip cookies while waiting for the others to return from school. I was now one of them. I was a big girl, learning to read and write while sitting in a desk in a straight row. Eyes fixed on the Queen every morning with her ruby red lipstick, pleasant smile and sideways pose. Singing God Save the Queen, followed by the Lord's Prayer until it was ingrained into our pintsized heads. These segments and flash backs of Grade One are unforgettable. But the trauma of attending the institution known as elementary school would be etched in my mind forever.

Miss Cook was classy and glamorous, with a beehive hairdo, matching skirts and jackets, go-go boots and frosted pink lipstick. She was my idol, my Grade Two teacher. Living only two blocks away from school, I could hardly wait to arrive, not because I was an eager, avid learner but because I looked forward to seeing Miss Cook. She could have been a model in the Sears or Eaton's catalogue. She spoke softly and was very kind. I was painfully shy and overly obedient. Every morning we gathered around Miss Cook's desk, waiting to find out who would be the chosen ones elected to remove Miss Cook's go-go boots. Sitting back in her chair, with her leg raised towards the ceiling, we (the two who were picked) with our stubby little hands, would grasp the heel and the toe of her boot and pull. Miss Cook would wiggle her toes and twist her ankle until finally the boot would slip off into our hands. With a sigh of relief, we would all feel accomplished from the completed task. After the daily boot removal, we (the class) would circle around Miss Cook's desk with our readers in hand and take turns reading aloud, sounding out the words with occasional prompts and gentle reminders from Miss Cook.

On one morning in particular as we gathered to read, I began to feel weak at the knees, my legs were shaking, and I could feel the blood drain from my face. Miss Cook took one look at me and asked me if I was okay. When I didn't answer, she instructed Kathleen Renton and Ellie Strom to run and get the janitor Mr. Magill. My best friend Mary wanted to be the one to go, raising her hand and jumping up and down. But Miss Cook never picked the exuberant ones so Mary had to stay behind in her spot around the teacher's desk. Miss Cook then sent me over to the back sink, in case I was going to throw up. With my head in the sink, the class went back to their Round Robin method of reading.

I could hear the monotone voices and syllables continuing to sound out the words as Lucky the dog ran with Sally and Peter. I persisted in suspending my head over the sink, mortified that Miss Cook could assume that I just might throw up in her presence. Eventually Mr. Magill made his way down to the primary wing. A large burly man with a handle bar moustache, quite stern but an impeccable floor polisher, as a rule he went about his business and paid no attention to the likes of us little Second Graders. And now here he was, picking me up, fire man style, throwing me over his shoulder in one fell swoop and packing me up the stairs, through the intermediate wing and down to the nurse's station. My mother was called and I was labelled with being a fainter. The doctor was called and then labelled me with being anemic, lacking iron. Thus began a long history of fainting, taking cod liver oil liquid and choking down cheap cuts of tough, unrecognisable meat for the iron content, to hopefully bring an end to my anemia and fainting spells.

Vince Bonner Bulldozing Ltd. and the kids

*Proud Vince and
his new Cat*

*Pushing some
dirt around*

The collapse of the Second Narrows Bridge, Vancouver

Karen playing it up for the camera

Dougie, Kenny, Karen, Linda

CHAPTER 11

Fish and Movies

The oppression of men and women of the 1950s was the catalyst for the 1960s peace and love generation. A cultural decade beginning around 1963 with the Kennedy assassination and ending around 1974 with the Watergate scandal, "The Sixties", is a term used by historians, journalists and other objective academics; in some cases, nostalgically spoken of as a revolution in social norms about clothing, music, drugs, sexuality and schooling. The social taboos relating to racism and sexism were the beginning of the monumental time in history known as the Women's Liberation Movement. Women's Lib: "Ban the Bomb and Burn the Bra"!! [32]

THE OUTCOME FOR ME GROWING UP IN THE 1960S WAS A RELA-tively happy childhood. My mother was on the PTA and did the bookkeeping for my dad's small business. She cooked and cleaned and paid the bills. My father worked hard running his small bull-dozing company, Monday to Friday, nine to five. They both curled and belonged to bridge clubs.

As the baby of the family, I had two older brothers and a much older sister. I liked to describe my oldest brother Dougie as the hippy, earthy type. He was artistic, tall, dark, and handsome. I loved my older brother and forced myself to call him Doug, because the name Dougie was for babies. Doug drank instant coffee out of a tall glass, with Coffee Mate. Later he would tell us how Coffee Mate was made from plastic, so then he started drinking his coffee black. He also said Colonel Sanders was mean to his chickens, and he then refused to eat meat anymore. He wore a brown suede jacket with fringes on it. My best friend Mary said that he looked like Neil Young. This made me proud and happy. One day he saw our cat lying under a tree, and when he laid down in the grass beside it to pet him, my brother realized that the cat had died. He said that the cat—Jet was its name—had turned harder than a board because rigour mortis had set in.

My other brother Kenny, who was closer in age to me, was also very handsome, but in a unique way from my eldest brother. I would refer to Kenny as my greaser brother, and in my mind that was a cool complement. My friend Mary said that this brother reminded her of Elvis Presley. And we all knew that Elvis the Pelvis was cool and groovy and simply out of sight. Sometimes Ken would tease me. My father hated teasing. He said that a person could die from being teased too much. I liked the attention my brother gave me, but I did not like being teased. Ken was very popular. He had blonde hair, blue eyes and a charming, mischievous smile. He always had lots of girlfriends, some of whom were nice. One of his girlfriends gave me her entire Barbie doll collection and another one gave me her report on the Roman Empire. Rather than just copy it, I handed it in directly as it was. I got a C plus. Again, the name Kenny was not grown up, so I forced myself to eventually call my brother Ken.

My sister was thirteen years old when I was born, and I did not get a chance to know her very well. She moved far away when she was seventeen, so I would have been four years old at that time. What I do remember is that she used to weigh her food on a little scale. She belonged to a group called Weight Watchers. My mother would go to meetings with her and after my mother herself lost weight she went shopping and bought a whole new wardrobe, beautiful dresses of all shades and styles. My father's favourite colour was yellow, so there definitely was a yellow dress in the mix.

My sister loved horses. She owned a horse and kept it at Laura Lynn riding stables in Lynn Valley. Her horse was white and its name was Tosca. She would ride her horse to our house, from Lynn Valley to Grand Boulevard where we lived in North Vancouver. We would all get a turn riding the horse up and down the lane. Sometimes my father would film us with his movie camera, riding Tosca in the lane behind our house. The best part was weeks later, after the Kodak film was developed. We would watch it on my father's big movie projector. Everyone would laugh, especially when he made the horse go backwards!

TO ME, MY FAMILY AND GROWING UP IN THE 1960S WAS COMpletely normal. We were neither rich nor poor. We always had yummy food. Regularly our breakfasts consisted of cinnamon toast and frosted flakes. Lunch would be Campbell's tomato soup, Clover Leaf tuna fish sandwiches, or Swanson's chicken pot pies. Dinners were my least favourite meal of the day. Sundays were roast beef and mashed potatoes. Mondays would be leftover roast in the form of a stew which my father said reminded him of the old days. Stew reminded me of dog food. If we had a dog, stew is what he would have eaten! The rest of the week would be hamburgers, pork chops, Shake & Bake chicken, and spaghetti, not always in that order. Occasionally we would be treated to Swanson TV dinners or Kentucky Fried Chicken from Colonel Sanders.

If we ever went out for dinner it had to be Mr. Mike's for steak and baked potatoes. The ultimate treat was a jug of root beer from the local A & W or a Mr. Misty slushy drink from the Dairy Queen. My mother loved orange pop floats. And she hated the Pillsbury dough boy. She baked her own bread, made chocolate chip and peanut butter cookies from scratch and simply loved Betty Crocker and Duncan Hines cake mixes. She always allowed me to help her bake and let me lick the spoon, which scarcely had anything on it as she frequently taught us not to waste.

Our clothes were always clean and rather crisp from the clothes line. Everything we wore was purchased from the Sears catalogue or bought at the Park Royal shopping centre, primarily from the Eaton's department store. We all had our own bicycles, birthday parties, and undivided attention when necessary. Our home was average in a working-class neighbourhood. The local school was two blocks away. Our house was adorned with black velvet paint-ings from Mexico, my parent's bridge tournament trophies, shag carpeting, two televisions, a hi-fi stereo, and a lazy boy recliner.

My father grew a vegetable garden in our backyard with tomatoes and green beans that would climb up the stucco wall for all to see. Before winter arrived, my mother and father together would can the cherries and pears that we picked from our own trees.

WE LOOKED FORWARD TO CAMPING TRIPS IN OUR CAMPER, VISITING my Uncle Hank in the Okanagan or the Van Acres camp site in Osoyoos every summer. Occasionally we would get a hotel stay at the Harrison Hot Springs resort and we would swim and swim in the naturally heated indoor and outdoor pools. On the drive home, my parents would buy fresh peaches for more canning at home and sometimes strawberries that we would pour cream over to lap up like the thirsty cats our family loved. We always had two or three cats roaming around.

Our favourite destination was always Uncle Hank's farm. He was our dad's brother, and he lived in Enderby with his wife, our Auntie Leona. They had four daughters, Waneta, Wilma, Roselie, and Tracy, our dearest cousins. My dad and Uncle Hank had both been raised very poor in the Depression Era, but they were completely different from each other. My dad was funny, loud, and outgoing, while Uncle Hank was kind, quiet, and reserved. He reminded me of the Hollywood actor Henry Fonda, while my dad looked much like James Garner from *The Rockford Files*.

Uncle Hank had been married to my Aunt Gladys, before he married Auntie Leona. They had divorced, but we never knew why. Gladys and Hank remained friendly, and always attended the same get-togethers, with no problems. They had two daughters, our older cousins Doreen and Marjorie. Marjorie lived in North Vancouver when I was growing up and everyone said that I resembled her. I loved hearing this because she was pretty and kind, she spoke softly, and smelled like carnations. She often gave me her hand me down clothes, and even if they were itchy or too big, I loved them anyway because they smelled like carnations, just like her.

MY PARENTS LOVED THEIR WAFFLE IRON, WHICH CAME OUT ONLY on the weekends. One morning after a feast of waffles and sausage, and after everyone had left the table, I sat quietly watching my mother stack each syrupy plate, one on top of the other. It crossed my mind that the bottoms of each plate were getting drenched in left-over syrup and how on earth were these plates ever going to come clean?

At that precise moment, my mother lifted the dishes up over her head and in one fell swoop, thrust them, syrup and all, onto the floor. The sound from the crashing force of dishes alarmed even herself. Exclaiming in an angry tone that was completely foreign to me, mother said "Why doesn't anyone help me around here?" as melted butter and maple syrup defiantly spat back up at her. Fortunately, the dishes were Corel Living Ware, so they did not break.

Being the only family member in ear shot, without responding, I leapt up from the table and ran to my bedroom, burying my head into my ballerina bedspread, and crying for what seemed like the rest of the day.

The very next day a great big box arrived from Simpson Sears. Inside was a square device on wheels. You could open a hinged door and put dirty dishes inside, roll it over to the sink, hook it up to the faucet and in one hour, hot and steamy clean dishes came out.

My mother's explosive outburst was never to be spoken of.

WE DID NOT GO TO CHURCH REGULARLY, PERHAPS ENOUGH TIMES to count on one hand. The time I do recall going to church, I remember wearing an Easter hat that had ribbons going down the middle of my back. My mother wore Marilyn Monroe type white gloves that travelled from her hand and went all the way to her elbow. They smelled like perfume, and they were soft. I loved them. She would often comment that she did go to church years ago because she was forced to. When she was nineteen years old she chose to stop going to the Catholic Church because she didn't like the idea of people confessing their sins to a priest and then going to the beer parlour to get drunk, swear, and beat their wives when they got home, only to then confess their sins to the priest all over again when the next Sunday rolled around. She said it was hypocritical. In fact, when my mother left her small town at the age of nineteen she not only left her church, she left her family too.

My father believed strongly in doing to others as we would have done to ourselves. He taught us to love our neighbours, and always explained that it did not matter what colour our skin was, we were all created equally. My mother strongly enforced never telling a lie and not swearing, although sometimes when she stubbed her toe, the occasional "s" word came out, which horrified and upset me, because it was so foreign to me.

GROWING UP IN THE SAME PLACE FROM BIRTH TO TWELVE YEARS of age, I got to know my neighbours and the many goings on in the neighbourhood. Mrs. Steveston, the lady next door to us, had the most amazing garbage. One couldn't help but notice the bright green stiletto heels poking out under the trash in her bin, or bottles of lightly used nail polish, discarded costume jewelry, and tea cups with daisy and rose patterns. Everything was so breathtakingly beautiful! Mrs. Steveston's back alley was definitely the one to watch on garbage pickup day. As the saying goes, one man's trash is another man's treasure. My mother was a little rattled at the idea of me picking through her friend's garbage, so eventually, much to my dismay and bewilderment, she kyboshed my weekly treasure trove expeditions.

The German lady, Mrs. Schmidt, who lived across the street, made the best home baked treats, and her granddaughter was another of my best neighbourhood friends. Elizabeth lived with her parents in the basement of her grandmother's house. Together our favourite pastime was doing cartwheels in her front yard in hopes of getting a homemade treat from her doting grandmother. If we tirelessly and repeatedly performed our routines, much to our relief, eventually Grandma Schmidt would come out of her house with a basket of something or other and off we would run, treat in hand, our mission accomplished.

Mrs. Wilson two doors down from us, allowed Mario and I to knock on her door and boldly ask for candy. In our clearest sing-song voice, we would call out "Can we have some candy?" We did this every day or so until my mother told us that it was not polite to ask for a candy. We were alarmed at my mother's announcement, as we had no idea that we were being the least bit rude. We truly believed that Mrs. Wilson was never annoyed and thoroughly enjoyed our visits and requests for candies. She always delivered upon our requests with a warm smile and never once ran out.

Another stop on our list of homes to visit was a little old lady that I never knew the name of. She was old and cute and lived in a miniature house with a garden that was twice the size of her house. She appeared to me like a doll, with a wrinkled up little face and twinkling eyes, always dressed in a beautiful but tiny full length gown. On one of our visits she took out of her closet a long black velvet cape that had a gold clasp and was completely lined with gold floral brocade. She handed me the cape, saying that I could get more use out of it than she ever would. I gladly accepted the glamorous gift. It became a super hero costume, a witch's cloak, and a royal shawl. I loved that cape more than anything, and eventually wore it out to the point of being frayed and tattered. She was certainly right about me getting a lot of use out of it. I rarely shared my prized possession with anyone else in the neighbourhood.

Aside from the familiarity and the routines of the neighbourhood, the most memorable were the block parties. There were at least two or three neighbourhood block parties a year. The ladies always wore pretty, floral dresses and the men crisp shirts with suits and ties. The suits were black and the shirts were always white. My parents referred to the gatherings as an "Open House." There were four houses in particular, ours being one of them, where neighbours would get together to eat, tell jokes, and laugh. Then the whole group would traipse over to someone else's house and do it all over again. The best "Open House" events were at Christmas. Swedish meatballs, garlic sausage, pickles, cheese and Ritz Crackers, French Onion Soup chip dip with ripple potato chips, and Dairyland eggnog would round out the feast.

Because my mother was almost forty when I was born, none of

her friends had children my age. By the 1960s when I came along, my parent's friends had already been married for twenty years, and had their children earlier. All their children were teenagers or adults by the time their parents were in their forties. Except for me, most of the neighbours had children who were the ages of my brothers and sister. During the Open House gatherings, the teenagers would go somewhere else when the joke telling and eating was going on. Except for me. I imagine that while the jokes were flying, the liquor was flowing, so that as time went on and people moved from house to house, everyone became quite looped. My mother and I seemed to be the only ones who were not drinking.

When the party moved over to our house, I walked into the living room to find my oldest brother singing while sitting on the couch. In true little sister fashion, I immediately told my mother that my brother was acting strangely and singing in the living room. As my mother investigated, we found that my teenage brother was drunker than a skunk (as my father referred to it). For the first time, at the age of eight, I saw what being drunk looked like. To me it appeared to be scary, and somewhat fun. My brother was sent downstairs to his bedroom to sleep it off, and the incident was never spoken of again.

THE WINTERS IN NORTH VANCOUVER WERE A FAR CRY FROM THE winters that my dad experienced in Saskatchewan and northern British Columbia. North Vancouver had never ceasing rain, while Saskatchewan and northern B.C. was below freezing with abundant snow. Weather memories were a topic that my father discussed with joy, and occasionally fear.

As he told it, the blowing snow storms on the Saskatchewan prairie could be deadly and breathtakingly beautiful at the same time. The extensive white terrain carried on for miles, the powdered snow blinding in the bright winter sunshine. Fence posts would peek out of the drifts, with snow caps on their heads. Sloughs and marshes would freeze over, and footsteps would be covered over with blowing snow, showing no trace of their existence. Scarves and mittens never were enough to keep one warm, and fingers and toes often became frostbitten.

The snow banks of Burns Lake would remain for months, piling up to the tops of the windows of homes and businesses. People were forced to dig paths from the doorways to the roads, woodsheds, and outhouses. They would stay indoors next to wood burning stoves, cozy, safe, and warm, with the comforting smell of fresh baked bread and a card game to keep everyone busy. The canned goods of summer sustained their existence during the long winters.

Every winter, my friends and I would pray for snow. I so wanted to experience the snow of my father's past. North Vancouver in winter was drenched in dreary rain. It was dark outside by 4:00 p.m. with hockey games on the television, steamy windows from cooking the supper, and drowsy faces falling asleep to the pitter patter of pelting rain.

It was both a comfort and a disappointment on Christmas morning to hear Bing Crosby swooning out the tunes of *White Christmas* and sentiments of *Walking in a Winter Wonderland*. *Sleigh Bells* and *Frosty the Snowman* were longed for, as brand new rubber boots, rain coats, and umbrellas were nestled under the Christmas tree, waiting for their users to jump in puddles all the way to school in January.

However, occasionally the barometer would dip, the weather would shift, and we would be blessed with a sufficient dumping of snow, glorious snow! Immediate trips would be made to the basements, garages, or hardware stores to get or purchase toboggans, crazy carpets, and flying saucers, our forms of transportation from the top of the hill to the bottom.

It was every man, woman, and child for themselves as we careened around other well-meaning sled riders, sliding and whizzing around obstacles, tipping over, rolling about and laughing until our bellies ached. Eventually we would climb back up the hill, dragging our form of transportation behind us to repeat the refreshing debacle again and again until we were called in for supper or bed or a favourite episode on television.

Waking up to a white front yard and the quiet calm that goes with it was every child's dream during the seasonal times in rainy Vancouver. Much to our great joy, we would be treated to a remarkable snowfall every second or third year somewhere between November and March. It was often unexpected and short lived.

My father would be the first out the door to begin the building of snowmen, snow angels, and even a snow dog replicating Snoopy from the popular cartoon *Charlie Brown*. The taller the snowman, the better, was my father's goal and motto. My job was making the face on my dad's human-like icy creation, so I would unearth stones for the eyes, pebbles for a pumpkin-like grin, and of course the notorious carrot for the nose. Sticks were used for the arms, preferably branches from an evergreen tree ripped free of its pine needles and shoved deep into the shoulder of our snowman. Larger rocks were placed as buttons that went up the front of the snowman's bursting frosty chest, and a scarf for his stubby neck (if one could be found or parted with). And finally, a photograph with someone's Kodak camera for proof of my father's prize-winning snow creation.

When not building masterpieces out on our front lawn, my dad would be taking us for snow mobile rides on Grand Boulevard. As a favourite client of Finning Tractor, he was given a demonstrator model of one of the first snow mobiles. This powerful, crazy snow blazer was completely unheard of to me and my neighbourhood friends. It was bright red, emblazoned with the name "Red Devil." As it was used only during rare circumstances when it snowed, I was proud to be hanging on tight behind my dad as he maneuvered down our snow padded city block on the infamous Red Devil, always stopping to pick up a stray kid or waving onlooker, laughing all the way, Jingle Bell style, as sung in the famous Christmas Carol.

EVERY LATE SPRING AND EARLY SUMMER MY FATHER WOULD TAKE my two brothers on a fishing trip. I was so sad to see them go, never suggesting that this was unfair, just sad to see them packing up the fishing rods and tackle, the canned meatballs, Coffee Mate, and cosy flannel beige and green sleeping bags. The inside of the sleeping bags is what was most interesting. There was a scene depicting boys with dogs shooting ducks and geese from the sky.

To make up for my forlorn expression and to get me away from the living room window, my mother had some rituals of her own. Once the boys and men drove off in the loaded down pickup truck, camper, boat and trailer, it was off to the movies for us girls who were left behind. The theatre, where every dream and fantasy could come alive, was always mesmerizing. I treasured my time with my mother, as my love of the silver screen took root and developed through my mother's eyes.

We had a 1967 green Impala. No seat belts, or they were there but never worn. There was no seat belt law in place at that time and I do believe they just got pushed through with all the dirt and dust balls. We never ate snacks in the car either, as we were rarely in a rush or ever had a need to do so. However, smoking WAS permitted and expected. An overflowing ash tray was always so full that the little pull-out drawer could never be closed. The windows were manually rolled up or down so a non-smoker could periodically stick their head outside, like a panting dog, for a quick breath of fresh air. Plastic, or rather vinyl seat covers, which protected the REAL original seats, were cold and uncomfortable. We would stick to them when it was summer and have a grand time sliding around on them in the winter. The fun part was a sharp right turn, causing the masses in the back seat to slide to and fro, back and forth, like a ride at the fair. An eruption of giggles from all the passengers followed, encouraging whomever was behind the wheel to repeatedly drive recklessly!!

Nothing was really frowned upon in those days in regards to driving rules and regulations. If one had a few too many at the beer parlour, the police officer would just give out a short verbal warning to get home and sleep it off, with a slap on the back and a little wink, wink, nudge, nudge. Horns were made for tooting hello and in my father's case he enjoyed driving past a bus stop, windows rolled down, squeezing his nose as he tooted the car horn. It looked like his nose was doing the tooting. This brought fits of laughter to myself, my friends, and the many innocent by-standers waiting for their bus.

Our route to the movie theatre, in our 1967 Impala, was over the Lions Gate Bridge. Living in North Vancouver we would go across town to downtown Vancouver only on special occasions like Christmas shopping at the Army & Navy, Chinese food in China town, and afternoon matinees at the Vogue theatre on Granville Street. On this noteworthy movie occasion, my mother was taking me to see the classic movie *Mary Poppins*.

My mother, an extremely careful and cautious driver (not having gotten her driver's license until she was twenty five) anxiously manoeuvred us out of our driveway, past Lonsdale and onto Marine Drive. Noticing that our gas tank was running low she meticulously pulled into a Standard service station, waiting patiently while the gas attendant cleaned our windshield, checked the oil and filled up our tank. Upon paying the attendant through the car window, my mother brightly put the car into drive and off we drove. Much to my mother's amazement the gas station attendant was hollering at us while waving his arms as we drove off. Noticing the commotion through the back window, I suggested to my mother that we stop the car. Slamming on the brakes, my mother soon realized that the nozzle of the gas pump was stilled lodged in the gas tank. By the time we drove off, gas was spurting out of the nozzle and the end of the hose had taken on the appearance of a wild snake flipping and flapping all over the place! This could have been a dangerous incident—thank goodness it wasn't! No harm done, other than leaving the gas station attendant bewildered at my mother's actions.

When all was said and done, my mother was hysterical with laughter and mortified with embarrassment. Following my mother's lead, I too was giggling as we headed for the Lions Gate Bridge. She loved referring to herself as another Lucille Ball. My mother's ability to laugh at herself and her foibles made her very appealing to everyone that she met. But on the other hand, she could be extremely intelligent and well versed in politics and in the know of most current events. She read the paper like it was going out of style. Stacks and stacks of newspapers were often brought to the beach, camping trips, and even visiting neighbours. She was always trying to catch up and would never part with her news.

Many years before our downtown movie matinee expedition, one would have to stop and pay a 50 cent toll to get across the water. For reasons unknown to me the toll had been abolished and we freely whizzed on, up and over the bridge through the Stanley Park causeway. Voila, just minutes into the core of our beloved city, our brand new 1967 Impala brought us to the cinema. The Hollywood show opened up a world of hopes and dreams. The drive itself was part of the fun and the outing was a glorious day with my mother. It was a very happy time growing up in the 1960s for a young girl with little expectations, living in the bubble of a middle-class world, raised by parents who had lived through the Depression.

Pulling into the Hudson's Bay parking lot, we drove and drove until we could find a suitable parking space. My mother always drove a far distance away from any concrete pillars and past other parked cars that could hinder her parking ability. She was a somewhat nervous driver but we always got where we needed to be and that was all that mattered to a six-year-old girl in 1966.

Perhaps we were both still stirred up from our previous mishap at the gas station or maybe it was the sheer adventure of being downtown, but what happened next stayed with my mother and me for the rest of our lives. My mother left the car running, with the keys in the ignition, without realizing it. We sat through an entire movie, cartoon, and previews without knowing that our car sat running in an undercover parkade at the Hudson's Bay Company in downtown Vancouver! All the doors were locked, the heat was blasting, and worst of all the keys were trapped inside the car. And we didn't find this out until we strolled back to the parking lot.

Rather than be mad or upset at the situation, my mother laughed. After discovering the car with the engine running, we sought out the parking lot attendant and he conveniently brought out a Slim Jim, an odd-looking metal crowbar-type tool. He carefully slipped the device into the door of our car. I do recall a smirk upon his face as if to say, "What a dumb broad." But he did get the window pried open and within seconds, the lock popped up like magic and he opened the door, reached in like a meticulous surgeon and turned off the ignition.

After we gathered ourselves, smoothed out our skirts, profusely thanked the hero, and took a deep breath, we slid into our seats and headed back to North Vancouver. The adventure had passed, the joy of the theatre a fresh memory and the merriment of being with my mother would stay with me always. The trip across town would not be complete without making a slight detour and stopping on the South side of the Park Royal shopping centre to enjoy our favourite meringue tart. This was another of my mother's rituals to complete our day at the movies. There was always room for a sugar filled treat.

THINKING BACK, MARY POPPINS WAS A TRUE INSPIRATION. I LOVED Mary Poppins with my entire essence of being, more than life itself. She was magical, beautiful, kind, and thoroughly captivating. I was pained knowing that she was not real. Even though I could never meet Mary Poppins, I still had my creativity and imagination, which I believed to be because I was left-handed. It was a known fact that left-handed people were creative, artistic, and smart in a different way than regular people. It was proven to me, as my older brother was left-handed too, and I once saw that he had drawn a running shoe that looked exactly like the actual shoe. My father started out as a left-handed person also, but back in the days of the Depression in the 1930s, they were strict, narrow minded, and a little bit crazy, so my father was forced to write with his right hand. Consequently, he struggled throughout his entire lifetime writing with the "wrong" hand.

My creativity led me to teach my friend Mario how to jump off of my playhouse in the back yard with an opened umbrella, half expecting to take flight and float upwards, hovering over our homes and entire neighbourhood, just like Mary Poppins. If "spit spot" were true, not only would I clean my bedroom with the snap of a finger, but I would also drift over with my opened umbrella, to clean my best friend Mary's bedroom too.

Inspired as I was by the movie *Mary Poppins*, it was the record album that my mother played over and over again (for both of us) on our hi-fi stereo system that sealed the deal. Knowing all the words to songs like "A Spoon Full of Sugar Helps the Medicine Go Down", "Supercalifragilisticexpialidocious", "I Like to Laugh" and the very sad "Tuppence", I could envision each scene unfolding as I sang myself to sleep every night with a contented smile on my face.

I suppose my fondness for Mary Poppins was unquestionably obvious to my family. For Halloween they dressed me as Mary Poppins, with a flower in my hat, a long skirt, and coat belted at the waist, and at my side, an authentic umbrella displaying a parrot for the handle. My older sister did my makeup—pink rosy cheeks and crimson red lipstick. I actually won a prize at the North Shore Winter Club's Halloween skating party. My prize was a bar of smelly soap. My pride at being Mary Poppins was the reason I won, for this I am sure.

For Christmas I received Mary Poppins jigsaw puzzles, four in a pack. Surely my obsession was short lived, at least until my next favourite movie came out, *Herbie the Love Bug.* How I tried to convince my parents to purchase a Volkswagen VW Bug! To no avail, as Chevrolet was the number one affordable, dependable vehicle for our family.

RETURNING HOME FROM THE FISHING TRIP WERE MY TWO BROTHers and father, tired and brimming with gratification. As tradition would have it, the fish that were caught and cleaned would be spread out on the front lawn on a bed of newspapers, for all to see. Neighbours would come from next door and a few doors down to help celebrate the catch. Pictures were taken, stories were told, and cats were shooed away as kids rallied around on their bicycles. A favourite part of the celebration was me being carried around in one of the handheld fishing nets. My toes would be all crunched up in the netting, but I would never let on how uncomfortable I was for fear that the treatment would end. I relished the attention from my father and enjoyed his hearty laugh as he toted me about the yard. Our family was the focal point on the day the men came home from fishing. I could feel the admiration and hear the swell in the voices that were fragmented with laughter and enthusiastic chatter.

Later that evening I overheard my father telling my mother that while on the trip, my brother Ken had gotten sick in the middle of the night. They had a long day and Ken, as active and energetic as he was, would not settle down for the evening. Finally, my father raised his voice, which he never did, and my brother quieted down and drifted off to sleep. He woke later, in the dark of night, in the middle of the bush, to throw up all over himself and the bedding. My father, being groggy and annoyed, grabbed him out of bed, changed the bedding and rinsed Ken off in the freezing cold lake. The whole time my brother remained quiet, not uttering a word as my father scrubbed him clean. All my father could hear was the deep silence of the woods and my brother's teeth chattering. When all was clean and back to normal my father put my brother quietly back to bed. There, in the dead of night, they all lay in the silence, hidden away in the safety of the camper. Out of the darkness, a small, shaky voice said, "I love yah dad." As my father communicated the story to my mother, he claimed that he held back the tears by biting his cheek, responding to my brother by saying, "I love you too Ken."

Perhaps he was remembering the unforgettable, frightening and lonely nights that he himself had once endured, when he had vowed to himself as a young boy never to raise his hand or utter an unkind word to any child that he may one day have, knowing that in the long run, he would raise a family of his own. He would be kind and gentle, never showing anger or rage as he had once seen and felt.

In my mind, my father was the King of the Castle. I often wondered if my friends knew that my dad was the best dad ever. I was ever so thankful to not have any of my friend's fathers instead of mine. Prideful jealousy would engulf me when the knock would come on our front door, and we would hear a chorus of voices all chanting "Can Mr. Bonner come outside to play?" My mother would respond "Perhaps after dinner he will come outside to play." The footsteps would clamour away only to return fifteen minutes later. This time my father would answer the door with his booming voice "What'cha want?" followed by his loud, light-hearted laugh. He would then run out the door, chasing and missing each child, their whoops of laughter and delighted screams trailing after the lot of them. I would stand on the front porch watching with a silly grin on my face, stretching from ear to ear, so proud that I had the best dad ever!

Off to the

movies

Enough fish
for all

Service with

a smile

Best

snowman

ever

Snoopy, Douglas and Frosty

CHAPTER 12

Don't Think Too Much

As we spend a good portion of our lives trying to figure out other people, what makes them tick and why they think the way they do, perhaps we should think more about ourselves and worry less about others.

My mother was a good example on how not to think too much, and how not to judge others or be bothered by them in the least. She was a highly intelligent woman, well read and up on current events, historical moments in time, politics of yesterday, today, and tomorrow. She would gladly drive my brother across town to picket the Vietnam War, happy to let him throw soap in the fountain of the court house with his hippy counterparts, and then proudly comment on how the suds caused quite a ruckus to onlookers and dignified folks passing by.

The rebellion, insubordination, and nonconformity became a hype and a huge part of the 1960s and '70s. It was a time of remarkable good fun and daring adventure for my mother, "making history" as she would call it. Sticking it to the man! This from a woman born and raised in the depression, marrying in an era when women stayed home with the children, while their men went off to earn the bread and butter or trudge off to war. Cooking, cleaning, and taking care of the children was done primarily by the women. In retrospect, three things that my mother was not particularly fond of or exceptionally good at was cooking, cleaning, and taking care of the children. But three things nevertheless that needed to get done. She completed these tasks to the best of her ability, which (as I found out years later) was much better than many other mothers of the day.

I and my three siblings always had a complete breakfast, lunch, and dinner and my mother was always there after school for us. We ate dinner at 5:00 p.m. sharp and bedtime was at 8:00 p.m. Refusing to purchase Velveeta processed cheese slices and eagerly investing in Betty Crocker cake mixes, my mother always ensured that we were clean, well fed, had bicycles, hula hoops, yo-yos, swing sets, and a peaceful, calm home. My father spiced things up with farfetched stories and tales that were always true, yet comical and endless, if not repetitive. This repetition I would come to love and eventually roll my eyes at, deep down wanting the monologue to continue but asking for it to please stop. At twelve years old, I was embarrassed on the outside but on the inside I was fondly memorizing each story.

When I was seven, 1967, girls were still not allowed to wear pants to school and we were not encouraged to play sports. "God saved the Queen" as the Lord blessed our days, and "Our Father Who Art in Heaven" was recited by all at Queensbury Elementary School. While I was shy, meek, and mild at school, dreading to be called upon, my mother was at home, busy taking care of the household. My father worked long hours, becoming well known in the community for his bulldozing company and expertise at getting a job done well with finesse and skill, the topsoil being his canvas and the excavator his paint brush.

AFTER WORK, AFTER SCHOOL, AND ON THE WEEKENDS, TIME WAS spent with family and friends. My sister was thirteen when I was born, so by the time she was seventeen (and I was four) she had moved out, taking with her the memory of Tosca and all the jaunts up and down the back lane.

My other experience with horses was when my father's Little League baseball team was in the local North Vancouver, Canada Day parade. To my pleasure and excitement, I was the chosen mascot, being pulled in a cart behind a mean, stubborn, yet very cute Shetland pony. Because my father was driving the pick-up truck with the entire baseball team in the back, he had given my mother the control of the movie camera from curb side. Her job was to document the entire parade with emphasis on myself and the Vince Bonner Bulldozing Little League team. As smart as she was, technology would not become her friend. As in most small-town parades, the cadence is based on the float ahead of you. If there is a break in the line-up, it is up to each individual float to speed things up and keep the ball rolling. This was important so the momentum would not drag and lag for the viewer's pleasure.

I was dressed in a bicentennial, frilly bikini, a pair of thongs (the flip flop, sandal type) and a banner across my chest, beauty pageant style, which read, Miss Vince Bonner Bulldozing Ltd. A fluffy little doggy fidgeted on my lap while I tried to manoeuvre my little-girl waving hand. I was struggling, smiling sweetly, and trying to keep everything in place. The boys from the baseball team all sat or stood in the back of the pickup truck wearing their clean, white striped baseball uniforms as my father proudly drove in an orderly procession. Handsomely, he waved and smiled that gorgeous smile of his for all to see.

We were all nothing short of a hit until the oohs and aws were drowned out by my crying and apparent dismay. The shaggy Shetland pony had his own agenda and decided to take a break, the kind that stops short, jerking and halting in a manner that in amongst all the waving, smiling, and dog holding, would dislodge my thong from my foot and knock it to the pavement below. It then became tangled in the spindly wheel of the cart, forcing the entire parade to dramatically come to a standstill.

As tears sprang to my eyes I was desperate not to disappoint the public's watchful eye and the praise and adoration from my father. These feelings would not be shaken for the rest of my childhood, following me long into adulthood, and many years later, with children of my own, "a people pleaser" would be my label.

Months later, as we once again gathered in front of the movie projector, we were able to re-live that eventful day. Wanting to capture the entirety of the moment, my mother scanned us all, the pickup truck, father, boys, myself, pony and cart all within a five-second timeline. We were forever replaying the scene to grasp the whole event within the blink of an eye. And yes, the best part was when my father so cleverly pressed the reverse button. I remember feeling disappointed with the lack of footage, but never once was I ridiculed for crying and we all only laughed at my mother's filming technique.

The Little League baseball team that my father so proudly sponsored would come to be known as Bonner's Dozers, the worst team on the league. With all my father's efforts, he was endlessly kind, without a competitive bone in his body. In the end the highlight of each and every game was Coke and treats my father would purchase at the local corner store as he still fondly drove the boys around in the back of the truck for all to see.

SUZY HOMEMAKER WAS A LINE OF MINIATURE TOY HOUSEHOLD appliances produced by Topper Toys in 1966. The toy line consisted of small ovens, little vacuum cleaners, refrigerators, and a few other items meant for little girls. There was also a Suzy Homemaker doll. The toys and doll were popular in the mid-1960s and into the early 1970s.

The term Suzy Homemaker eventually became an insult directed at women who were judged for being excessively domestic. I, on the other hand, wished for a Suzy Homemaker mother, and I too wanted to be a Suzy Homemaker mother when I grew up. Neither happened.

For some reason, I thought that everyone else's mother was a Suzy Homemaker type. Meaning that they cooked, cleaned, sewed costumes, and knitted luxurious sweaters, made crafts, decorated cakes and the family home for all festive occasions.

In my mother's defense, she did try. Like the time she took Chinese cooking lessons to prepare a beautiful Chinese dinner for my brother's birthday. After all the grocery shopping, and spending all day in the kitchen slicing, dicing, mixing, and sautéing only to have the entire meal gobbled up in less than ten minutes, my mother said, "Never again." We went back to having KFC and store-bought birthday cakes from then on for all other birthday celebrations. She too wanted to be the Suzy Homemaker breed, but deep down inside, being a private detective or living the life of a journalist were her true passions.

Fay Emberly, Mrs. Salsback, and my cousin Marjorie were to be my mother's go-to people for anything remotely crafty or creative.

Fay Emberly was an elderly woman who smoked like a chimney, and upon entering her home, one could be either enamoured or horrified by the yellowing décor of nicotine-infested ancient furniture layered in doilies and exquisitely dressed dolls. The doilies were pink, blue, yellow, and cream. The dolls usually had an eye or two missing, were in need of a better hairstyle, and were adorned in fancy, embroidered or knitted gowns with intricate lace details, which Fay had made. She even sewed Barbie Doll clothes. There were also table cloths, pillow cases, slip covers, and anything else you could stick a needle into and come up with a design of hand-stitched fruit, flowers, baskets, and bows. All of these were made with assorted colourful threads.

I enjoyed our little visits to Fay's house, and always hoped that she would give me a Raggedy Ann and Andy doll. She made those too, and they were amazing. Red yarn for a shaggy mop top of hair, overall for Andy and matching dress and apron for Ann. Their faces were stitched with embroidery, depicting happy grins and surprised expressions. My mother always whispered to me that they were far too expensive, so I did not get one, although I asked regularly.

Fay had a gruff smoker's voice and an even gruffer hacking cough. One of her eyes was a bit distorted and used to weep down the side of her face. I always hoped that she would take one of her many delicate hankies and dab away at the liquid that oozed out of her like an open wound. She never did. She was not really friendly, and perhaps she was offended at how I would pull the collar of my shirt up and over my nose and mouth, so I didn't have to breathe in the constant second-hand smoke. It was a common way of coping when around a heavy smoker inside a car or a confined space of any kind. Children everywhere could be seen as headless bodies, mouths covered in a conspicuous manner to protect their lungs, or at least to make a statement against smoking. Our visits ended with my mother getting advice about something or other and once in a while I would get a knitted Barbie Doll hat for twenty-five cents.

MRS. SALSBACK WAS A LADY FROM MY MOTHER'S BRIDGE CLUB. She was also a seamstress, working out of the basement of her home. Her specialties were a fabric called seersucker, and stretch double knit polyester, which were apparently very tricky to sew with. My mother thought that Mrs. Salsback was an artistic genius, a mastermind of the sewing machine. Many a Saturday afternoon, I stood perched on a stool so I could be measured, poked, and prodded for a handmade new outfit. She always wore her own homemade pantsuits in greens and yellows and the latest trendy glasses that practically covered her entire face.

The downstairs of her house had everything a dressmaker needed: the latest Singer sewing machine, tissue paper patterns, extra sharp scissors, and measuring tapes draped over chairs. My favourite item was the sewing kit with the cutest little tomato pin cushions. I always wanted one and thought how perfect they would be as a little bedside table for my Barbie Dolls. My favourite outfit that Mrs. Salsback made for me was a pantsuit with bell bottom legs and a snap-up jacket. It was a stretchy fabric with bright orange and white stripes. I felt very modern and posh every time I wore it.

Our time with Mrs. Salsback ended after a fainting incident. She had the habit of talking on the telephone and forgetting about me as I stood up on the stool waiting to be measured or pinned or both. Apparently, I was already anemic and prone to fainting spells, but my mother did not want to force food down my throat because she hated it when her mother did that to her. So long story short, after standing for far too long, combined with my anemia and lack of fluids, I fainted in Mrs. Salsback's basement in amongst patterns, fabric, and pin cushions. I think my mother and I were both relieved to be done with Mrs. Salsback.

Another fainting spell that I will never forget was when my oldest brother Doug offered to take me to the comic book store on Marine Drive. I was so excited and honoured by his offer that I gladly said yes and off we went. Once inside the small, intensely warm and over-crowded shop, the room began to spin and just as my surroundings started to turn silver and grey, my brother whisked me outside to the curb where he sat me down and made me put my head between my knees. This I learned, was a well-known technique for a fainting attack. I asked my brother if I could die from fainting and he said no. I was so amazed and flattered that he knew exactly what to do. I was cured within minutes, but no comic books were purchased that day.

MARJORIE, MY FAVOURITE COUSIN, WAS MY MOTHER'S THIRD GO-TO person. As a wedding present, my dad had bulldozed and cleared the lot that their house stood on. They even had a goldfish pond in the front yard, which my dad dug up for them too.

Marjorie could do anything. Her home was impeccable and modern. Every Christmas, she and her husband had a theme for their Christmas tree. One year they would have all red lights and red tinsel, and another year they would have all green, or blue. Candy dishes and coasters and all the right stuff lined coffee tables and fireplace mantels. They had ornaments all over their house, mementos from their trips to Hawaii or crafts that Marjorie had made in her ceramics class. One of my cherished items was a ceramic potato with a lid, where you could put sour cream inside for your baked potato. Marjorie also took a cake decorating course, so she could decorate just about anything: cakes, cookies, cupcakes, and those tiny little miniature cakes called petite fours. But the best part of Marjorie's talents was her ability to make ice skating costumes for me.

I had taken figure skating lessons at the North Shore Winter Club for some time, and every year there was a show that all the classes would be in. Many efforts went into putting these ice carnivals together, especially by the parents. As they rallied together to discuss costumes and themes, sequins and fabric, my mother would be in the viewing area, reading a book. All the information was gathered and then carted off to Marjorie's. Between Mrs. Salsback's, the comic book store incident, and now standing on yet another stool at Marjorie's house, my mother urged me to eat more meat for the sake of iron content, to combat the fainting spells.

This was always a battle, but I dutifully gnawed away at ground round drenched in ketchup, and plugged my nose to get it down.

I proudly showed up at dress rehearsals in the most striking ensemble. Each outfit was made from satin and lined with flannel (most of the other girl's suits were not lined). As I glided around the ice, I felt well put together and confident going into my shoot the duck. The first year I was dressed as a cowgirl boot with a silver fabric spur on my back side. The second year I was a Christmas ornament with a handmade bobble for a hat. The last year of my figure skating experiences, I was a Queen's Page.

It was this last year that my parents brought my friend Mary to the show. She was so excited to see me when I stepped out onto the ice that she yelled my name as loud as she could. As I proudly looked up into the crowd to spot my friend, I lost all my concentration and balance, which caused me to fall flat on my face. Scrambling back up to my feet, I carried on with the routine, as the show must go on.

THE POPULARITY OF HAVING A WEEKEND COTTAGE, A FAMILY getaway, was a growing trend. With my sister practically an adult, working in a bank, and my brothers and mother losing interest in camping, it was thought that we would all benefit greatly from a home away from home. Two choices that my parents came up with were property on Pender Island on the Sunshine Coast, or fifty acres of land further east, out in the valley in a place called Mission. Without any involvement or input from the family, the decision was made. My parents would purchase fifty acres of land for a whopping price of $16,000 dollars, much to the dismay and opinions of friends, neighbours, and business associates all throwing in their two cents worth, that my parents had spent far too much money on a desolate parcel of land in the middle of the bush.

My father's intention and eventual completion was to partially log the land, using the logs to build a log house, log barn, and corral for horses. Three ponds with natural springs would be excavated and dug out for swimming, two of the ponds being stocked with rainbow trout for fishing, and one pond near the barn to be accessible water for the livestock. The project brought everything my father loved about his past, and his physical labour, together for all to enjoy.

This was to be true for the most part. My oldest brother would be involved in the designing of the cabin, both brothers helped build, my Uncle Hank assisted in the purchase of a small sawmill, even living with us for a time to help with the work and operation of it, and I once again enjoyed time alongside my father. We travelled back and forth from North Vancouver to Mission every weekend upon weekend, often stopping along the way to pick up a bucket of Colonel Sanders Kentucky Fried Chicken. While my father worked at building, clearing, and living out his dream, I spent many lazy days drifting in the pond, floating on the raft he had created for us, drifting and diving to my heart's content. I ate fried egg sandwiches doused in ketchup for breakfast and explored the afternoons away while befriending the neighbour's dog. In the evening we played charades with my father as he stoked the wood stove with crackling cedar bits and long burning logs that he cut and stacked effortlessly behind the newly constructed rustic log home.

On many occasions my best friend Mary would accompany us, which only added to the delight of a weekend away with my dad. Mary's carefree, spunky nature kept us busy creating games, trying to capture the neighbour's horse and even doing so only to fall off into the barbed-wire fencing! Mary, the risk taker, always received cuts and scrapes that my father would doctor and treat without any annoyance or reprimand.

However, not realizing the magnitude of what was next, a dark cloud loomed, foreboding of what was to come. Happy and eager as my father was, my mother was not. I do not recall her joining us on these weekend trips to the property, the "farm" which the fifty-acre property became known as. My mother did not share in my father's dream, aspirations, and the passion that he felt for the land he had purchased and successfully developed. She thought they had achieved so much up until then, residing happily in a beautiful, scenic, flourishing city and creating a life with many friends, raising four children and even acquiring a membership to the North Shore Winter Club (an honorary membership that my father acquired after clearing and developing the land), a country club with swimming lessons, hockey tournaments, and skating carnivals.

My mother felt that they were digressing, moving back in time, back to the days of the Depression Era, poverty, and long-forgotten painful memories, days that they had painstakingly moved away from. Dirt, trees, and hard labour that were thought to be a thing of the past, were now back. The purchase of the land on Carr Street in Mission, B.C. would be the beginning of my mother's own deep dark depression, the tip of the iceberg, the unknown lurking demon of mental illness.

These carefree happy times would be forever interrupted.

DURING THE TRUDGING BACK AND FORTH TO THE PROPERTY, I HAD become lost in my own little world. When I was nine I asked my mother if I could go to church. My mother said, "There is a church across the boulevard, why don't you go there?" She then decided to go with me my first time to ensure that it was not a cult. We attended the chosen church one warm and sunny Sunday morning in early May. After paying close attention to the sermon, mom decided that I would be fine going on my own. For the following three years after our first visit, off I would go, by myself, to Sutherland Bible Chapel located a short walk from my home at the top of Grand Boulevard in North Vancouver.

I loved it there. Every Sunday I would sit in the front row with all of the other children. After the singing had ended, all the children would be herded off to Sunday school which was located in the basement of the church. The best part about Sunday school was Mrs. Steele my Sunday school teacher. Her shoulder-length brown hair was back combed into a swooping side part that swirled up at the end into a beehive hairdo. She wore floral dresses and pumps, a pearl necklace that set off her creamy white complexion, and she spoke like an angel from heaven, soft, kind, and encouraging. She smelled like our next door neighbour's flower garden, the kind you were told not to pick, but did so anyways.

The part of Sunday school that I did not like was having to memorize Bible verses. I never felt like a very clever student during elementary school, continuously thinking that everyone else in the classroom was much smarter than me. This way of thinking carried over into my Sunday school days as well. It felt hard and rather daunting to painstakingly read verses, to remember words and phrases that I did not clearly understand. The good book was not read or enforced at home so rarely did I crack open the white leather Bible that I begged my mother to buy for me. It was a beautiful Bible with a gold zipper and little gold cross to pull the zipper open and closed with, like a secret compartment so one could store church bulletins or my best friend Mary's picture. This glowing white Bible soon became my most treasured possession. Carrying it under my arm, off I would traipse early Sunday morning across the dewy grass to church, while the rest of the world lay fast asleep.

As Sundays would come and go, there I would be alone, void of verse, walking through the doors of the chapel. Taking in the view of each smiling family, children firmly grasping onto their parent's hands, fathers carrying the babies while shaking hands and nodding as people settled into their seats. Just when my feelings on the whole church atmosphere began to wane, some brilliant Bible scholar brought in the point system. It was announced during the service that a store, a small kiosk with prizes and nic-nacs had been installed in the basement, and as of that day, each memory verse would be worth points. The points could be used like money in the little store. One could purchase a Biblical comic book, a candle, or perhaps a small notebook. We were then taken in groups to tour and view the new addition to our whole Sunday school experience. That's when I saw the pin—the silver bird of peace pin with its wings out-stretched, perfect for the lapel of any jacket, sweater, or blouse. I had to have that pin. The following Sunday, after spotting the pin, I managed to memorize the now long forgotten verse that enabled me to acquire the points that would be my ticket to purchase the simple but divine pin. What turned out to be better than obtaining the pin, was the look of sheer joy and pride on Mrs. Steele's serene face when I boldly and confidently recited my memory verse. I do believe that there were honest to goodness tears welling up in Mrs. Steele's eyes. I wore my pin with pride and in the lazy, hazy days of the hippy movement in the late 1960s, I relished my reply when anyone would ask me about the pin I so proudly wore. "It is called The Bird of Peace," is what I confidently boasted for anyone in earshot.

My mother once said to me, "I can't understand why there is so much fussing and fighting over religion, aren't we all just trying to get to the same place?" She believed in God and told me that she prayed. However she grew up in a time where church was a place to repent of the sins from the past week, and receive a free pass or ticket to sin again. Sunday, during my mother's childhood, was always just around the corner, where one was washed clean. A confession and a Hail Mary or two would do the trick to enable the vicious circle to continue.

My mother found church to be somewhat hypocritical. But not my church. My church was all loving, all forgiving, and based on Jesus. "What would Jesus do?" was a popular quote, and we all tried hard to 'love thy neighbour', 'be kind', and 'do unto others'...and the list goes on. When I brought home the church bulletin with up and coming events, I was anxious and excited to inform my mother about Day Break Bible Camp on Anvil Island. I wanted to go. Open-mindedness was a huge trait of my mother's. She thought that Bible Camp was a grand idea. She approved and that was all that mattered. My mother paid the bills, did the shopping, cooked the meals, maintained the house, and made the decisions, which my father agreed with whole heartily. Everything and anything my mother put forth my father willingly said yes to in the most positive of ways. Perhaps behind closed doors there was more of a discussion between my parents, a decision-making tryst, but not to the knowledge of myself and my siblings. To us, mom was the head of the household and dad backed her 100%.

The list of what to bring to summer camp had boxes to tick off, things to purchase, pack, and find. The first step was a visit to the Army and Navy on Hastings Street in downtown Vancouver. My pride and joy (next to my white Bible) was my brand-new orange sleeping bag with flower power, pink and yellow flowers delightfully printed on the fabric. It was what the hippies called psychedelic. Not only was the colour wild but the inside was lined with pink flannel to ensure a warm, cosy nights' sleep. A flashlight and new bathing suit concluded our visit to the Army and Navy, a considerably special trip, as it was the store that we usually only frequented at Christmas time.

The toiletries, shampoo and soap, were squirted into miniature, plastic containers that were specifically designed for travel. A new toothbrush and toothpaste completed the list.

My bag was packed, every box had been ticked and we were once again headed across town, this time to the ferry terminal near the Bay Shore Hotel. I said my goodbyes as I climbed aboard the boat, alone, brave, and wondering what I had got myself into. During the two-hour cruise, I sat by myself and munched on my tuna fish sandwich and drank my orange pop that my mother had packed for me. According to the list, a sack lunch was mandatory. Box ticked.

I eyed my fellow passengers, admiring the camaraderie they all shared. Girls strolling about the ship's deck arm in arm, heads thrown back laughing, giggles and fresh faces looking forward to six glorious days of adventure, crafts, archery and unknown to me, church and Bible study twice daily.

Much to my surprise, I was approached by a trio of girls at least two years older than myself. Perhaps they felt sorry for me or perhaps my forlorn expression made me an easy target. One will never know. They did become my fast and furious friends; even if I did not particularly think so, they did. By the time the boat docked at Anvil Island my new-found friends had convinced me to ask permission to be in their cabin. They helped me by begging and cajoling the camp director, they pouted and stated that I knew no one, nor did I have even one friend. They promised to take diligent care of me. We were placed in cabins according to our age, for obvious reasons such as maturity levels, a common ground, an overall understanding of each other's likes and dislikes—many reasons for which I should not have been placed with a trio of girls that were older in ways other than just chronologically!

They were mean to our camp counsellor by putting broom sticks in her bed. She cried and I felt horrible because I liked her very much. They bullied a lovely Asian girl who, like me, had no friends. Her name was Marlene, and she was shy and meek with the most beautiful hair I had ever seen. We both shared a dislike for the trio, became friends, and eventually pen pals until Marlene's mother died and she stopped writing. She was from Washington DC.

One afternoon after lunch, I and the trio were hauled off to the nurse's station. The nurse showed us pictures of people with brain damage and the outcome and dangers of sniffing glue. I had no idea what the nurse was talking about and only found out later that the trio had been sniffing glue and pulled my name into their dramatic escapades. I never spoke up or even redeemed myself. I did not seek out the nurse or my camp counsellor to explain my innocence. I should have tried to transfer to another cabin with girls my own age, who still played with Barbie dolls and won prizes in their church stores. But I didn't. I had Marlene, my new cosy sleeping bag, Jesus in my heart as I crossed my fingers every night, in hopes that Satan would not get me while I was sleeping.

Sit-Downers Arrested in B.C.

Picketing in downtown Vancouver

The log house in Stave Falls, Mission, B.C.

CHAPTER 13

Nine Lives

There is an ancient proverb that claims, "A cat has nine lives. For three he plays, for three he strays, and for the last three he stays." Some people believe the nine lives myth is related to the cats' ability to always land on their feet. Cats are also known for their dexterity and agility. Cats can survive things that are severe enough to kill them. [33]

WHEN I WAS TWO, AS THE STORY GOES (WHICH IS NOT FROM MY own memory), my father had a life-threatening fall down a one-hundred-and-sixty-foot canyon. He survived, and in doing so coined the phrase from family and friends, "Vince Bonner has nine lives," having escaped death in numerous circumstances under various conditions.

It had rained all night. Torrential rain in North Vancouver can cause flooding, power outages, dark days, and blacked out nights. In 1962 Vince had established himself as a business owner of his small bulldozing company and due to his intense work ethic, and his dynamic and charismatic personality, he was a very popular man within the community. He was often called on from the

City—the Municipality, to perform bulldozing jobs, clearing land, attending meetings, and occasional handyman jobs of sorts.

A call came in at 9:00 in the morning, when Vince would not usually have been found at home. But due to the heavy rains the night before all excavating and lot clearing had been called off for the day. Rain and dirt do not mix well in the bulldozing business. Once you start messing around with a 40-ton piece of equipment sitting atop amalgamated, rain drenched dirt, all you come up with is a soggy mass of mud, resembling Mrs. Bonner's Duncan Hines cake batter. The inevitable outcome would be thousands of dollars socked into pulling a stuck Cat out of the job, or waiting until the spring to dislodge the equipment. The phone call was a request for Vince to take a drive over to the Lynn Canyon Suspension Bridge. Apparently, the rain storm from the night before had caused monumental damage to the entrance of the suspension bridge. A tree had fallen and there was a safety risk to the bridge and any person wanting to cross it.

"The construction of the bridge was completed in 1911 as a private venture. It is 50 meters in length and 160 ft. high from the bottom of the canyon. Lynn Canyon Park and the suspension bridge were officially opened at the first Lynn Valley Days celebration September 14, 1912. The Lynn Creek and Lynn Valley area are named after sapper John Linn who was granted land at the mouth of the creek in 1871. In 1910 the McTavish brothers donated 5 hectares of their canyon land to the District of North Vancouver. The district accepted the gift and added another 4 hectares. Designs for the Lynn Canyon Suspension Bridge were created by civil engineer and architect, C.H. Vogel. As a private operation, the suspension bridge cost 10 cents per person to cross. Later the fee was reduced to 5 cents, but the bridge fell into disrepair and was finally closed.

The district of North Vancouver eventually made repairs and reopened it, free to everyone." [34]

It was the district that contacted Vince, so off he went on that soggy morning in his Ford pickup truck to inspect the damage, taking with him his foreman Roy. There was a short hike into the trail head and soon enough Vince and Roy discovered a two foot by twenty-foot cedar tree which had fallen directly on top of the entranceway to the bridge. With power saw in hand Vince climbed out onto a tree limb and began to saw away at the caught-up menace. The instability of the tree combined with the rain-drenched, mossy embankment caused Vince's section of the tree to slip. In one fell swoop the tree broke free, sending Vince, power saw in hand, and the tree shortly thereafter, to plummet 100 feet, landing on a ledge below.

In complete shock, Roy called down to Vince, and when there was no response, Roy ran back to the parking lot where a pay telephone awaited him. Calling 911, Roy explained to the dispatcher the situation and asked for immediate help. While awaiting assistance, Roy returned to the edge of the cliff, anxiously peeking over. To his horror and surprise he came face to face with the bloody face of Vince who had climbed, super hero style, back up the side of the rock face! As Vince hoisted himself up and over the escarpment, Roy gasped and straight away fainted. When the ambulance arrived Vince was trying to revive Roy as the paramedics proceeded to place Roy on the stretcher. In all the commotion, Vince became dizzy with a severe concussion and as Roy came to, he was able to explain to the responders that they had the wrong man on the stretcher. Immediately Vince was tended to and off they went to Lions Gate Hospital.

Family members and the Vancouver Sun newspaper were contacted, Vince's fall down the side of the canyon making headlines and highlighting a supportive, relieved family at his side. To no one's surprise, Vince made a full recovery. However, some deafness did occur, which ended up being the bane of the family's existence, forcing them to yell their conversations from here on in. The volume on the television was kept permanently on high, and Vince suffered with a terrible ringing in his right ear in exchange for a good deed. All would be well and good with eight lives still left for this invincible man's journey.

The drama and the dust settled. The rains dried up and life went back to normal in the Bonner household; block parties, fishing trips, camping trips, weekends away at Harrison Hot Springs, card games, the PTA, hot dog days, the dentist, Little League, movie theatre nights, and Chinese food in Chinatown. The 1960s was a time of family: *Leave it to Beaver*, *I Love Lucy*, and games of monopoly, the 6 o'clock news with Walter Cronkite, hippies, the Vietnam War, and "Can Mr. Bonner come out to play?"

CONTINUING WITH HIS BULLDOZING BUSINESS, VINCE WAS BECOM-ing more well-known and very well liked in the community of North Vancouver. Soon enough though, the rain would cause Vince to almost lose another of his nine lives.

He was called on by the District to do some bulldozing work up the dry creek bed of Mosquito Creek which lead up to the Capilano River. After a long warm summer, it was the perfect time in the season to clear some boulders and debris to open up the lower basin so the reservoir above could spill into the basin below.

Construction for the Cleveland Dam was started in 1951 with its completion date of 1954. Located at the head of the Capilano River in North Vancouver, British Columbia, Canada, the concrete dam, also known as the Capilano Reservoir, stores a portion of the Lower Mainland's drinking water. One can walk across the dam and observe the river and the spillway free of charge.

Formed above the dam, Capilano Lake stores the river's waters, stretching north for more than five kilometres. The lake is one of three major watersheds in the GVRD and it currently supplies forty percent of the region's drinking water.

About five hundred meters below the dam is the Capilano Fish Hatchery. The hatchery offers basic education about the life cycles of the fish, with educational displays that explain spawning and the work that is done at the Hatchery.

The rugged waters of the Capilano River within the park also attracts kayakers and canoeists with a variety of hiking and biking trails. The park has also been used for film and television productions.

The dam is named after Ernest Albert Cleveland, who served as the first chief commissioner of the Greater Vancouver Water District from 1926 until his death in 1952. It was Ernest Cleveland who felt the need for an efficient water supply as well as a sustainable use of water resource. [35]

After about a week's worth of work on the dry riverbed, it unexpectedly began to rain. Vancouver is one of Canada's rainiest cities, with over 161 rainy days per year. However, it had been a particularly dry season so as the weather drastically changed, so did the water levels at the reservoir. Unbeknownst to the District, Vince, and his employees, the rain would soon become torrential.

Vince was awakened in the middle of the night by the shrill ring of the telephone. On the other end an incomprehensible voice that could barely be made out exclaimed that Vince only had a few short hours to get his bulldozer out from below the dam. They were calling for a state of emergency, that the dam be released due to heavy rain and the dramatically rising reservoir. Vince, with his foreman Roy in tow, hurriedly made it to the site below the dam.

The dense pelting rain made visibility almost impossible. Climbing down into the canyon, Indiana Jones style, Vince and his foreman made it to the Cat in breakneck speed. Revving up the enormous piece of heavy duty equipment, the two men began crawling the bulldozer and themselves methodically out of harm's way. Unable to see clearly, they only managed to make it a couple of hundred feet when the warning sirens began sounding. There was no more time, the dam was about to be released.

With water now cascading from the gates of the dam above, emerging from the darkness came a voice hollering instructions. A life raft was being thrown down to them, they must leave the bulldozer and run for their lives. Searchlights were now cascading light on high as the raft banged and bounced towards them from the side of the canyon overhead. Waist-deep in swirling icy water, the two men managed to flee towards the raft. Within seconds they had thrust themselves aboard and were careening down the rapids as if all hell had broken lose.

At one point Roy yelled to Vince, "I can't see! I can't see!" When Vince looked down he saw his buddy's spectacles barely hanging from a flailing rope that was attached to the raft. Vince, hero style, grabbed the glasses as the raft began to steady itself and float to the mouth of the river, somewhere down around Park Royal. With what seemed like minutes to spare, the men were safe. Unfortunately, the bulldozer was not. Pulverized from the force of the water and the down-pouring of rocks, dregs, and sediment, it was not rescued from its watery grave until the following spring, unrepairable.

My father the superstar.

THE NEXT LIFE OF VINCE BONNER'S TO BE TAKEN AWAY WAS ON A sizzling summer night in mid-August. The family had just returned from their yearly vacation in the Okanagan, visiting Uncle Hank and Auntie Leona and their four daughters, our cousins, Wanetta,

Wilma, Roselie and Tracy. Travelling six hours with the camper and pickup truck to the land of dry warmer temperatures, fresh fruit, tomatoes and sweet corn was the highlight of the whole summer. The family visit to see favourite relatives was often combined with a camping trip to the Van Acres campsite in Osoyoos. This was always a summer tradition and a memorable experience for all—air mattresses, motor boat rides, sunburns, canned meatballs, comic books, and campfires contributing to the memories.

Upon returning home from vacation, Vince felt the need to go straight to work. Summer was a busy time in the construction business, especially in often rainy Vancouver. When the sun shone brightly so did the work and so did the bank account. It was on an early evening just after dinner that Vince had to head back out to a job he had recently started, a lucrative, important job. It was a lot that he was clearing for a church being built just off the Upper Levels Highway near Lloyd Avenue. Vince needed to rev up the Cat, push in the fire, check on the fire watcher, and return home. As most jobs go for Vince, in the middle of summer, it was necessary and easy enough.

Walking out the back door with a full belly from the evening supper and down the path towards his pickup truck, he heard faint chanting. What started faint, soon erupted into fits of laughter with a louder sing song of, "Can Mr. Bonner play with us?" A request that I had heard many times over, it was the neighbourhood children asking if they could play with my dad. Sometimes they would arrive in droves, ringing the doorbell, calling out to him as he drove past on the street, and even sending notes to my mother asking if Mr. Bonner could come out and play. My parents thought that it was funny, and deep down inside I was so proud knowing in my heart that I had the best dad ever. Every so often, the green-eyed monster called jealousy would show its ugly head, but most times I could keep everything under wraps and join in the chanting.

On this night as he was rushing out to work, he stopped and took a moment to hurriedly play the game Dog Pile. He would lie on the ground, face down while ten, fifteen, and even twenty children would pile on top of his back. On the count of three he would raise up off the ground with every ounce of strength that he could muster, letting out a loud growling sound. Upon fully standing, children would be flung everywhere, each flying and rolling to the grass. One boy even landed in one of our cherry trees! Always laughing, the kids would cry out for more, more, more, again, again, again!

Work was beckoning Vince, so he had to leave the children in the back yard after only one game. He eagerly ran down another flight of stairs to the back parking lot just off the lane. Trailing after him was me, asking if my friend Valerie and I could go to work with him. We were both eight years old and my father used to call us The Gold Dust Twins. He said sure, and we all piled into the truck. As we drove off towards Grand Boulevard and the highway we could still hear the neighbourhood kids chortling and sputtering in fits of laughter from the previous game. Reaching the work site, my dad hopped on his bulldozer, revved it up and began pushing the slow embers together. Jumping down off the Cat, he then grabbed the power saw and sawed a few of the stray bits of tree branches, throwing them in a heaving motion onto the fire. Within minutes we were back in the truck and on our way home.

It was shortly after leaving the site, while my dad was driving, that I noticed he was rubbing and stretching out his right arm like it was sore. He then began to clutch his chest and that's when I knew something was wrong. Valerie and I became very quiet as I carefully asked my dad if he was okay. At the precise moment my question came out, he pulled the truck over and jumped out, leaving his door open and the engine running. He was staggering and running down the sidewalk into a nearby home. He flung the door open and dashed inside. I found out later that my dad knew of a doctor who lived there. The doctor took one look at my dad, recognizing him, and he knew right away that Vince Bonner was having a heart attack. With his doctor's bag handy he pulled out a needle and gave my father a shot of adrenaline. Right then and there my father was having a heart attack and this doctor was saving him. Soon an ambulance was called, my friend and I were driven home in the still running truck, by another neighbour, and my mother drove off to the hospital to meet the ambulance as it arrived.

Stress, high cholesterol, over-eating, and over-exertion all played a key role in my father's heart attack. Another life was saved, and thank goodness for his nine lives because he still had six left. I knew that Vince Bonner was invincible, he would live forever and continue to beat the odds.

TIME ROLLED ON AS IT ALWAYS DOES—SWIMMING LESSONS, SKATING lessons, summer camps, Hallowe'en costumes, trick or treating for miles and miles, Christmas concerts and Christmas decorations; sliding down closed off, snow-covered streets, presents and New Year's resolutions. With the 1970s came Sonny & Cher, Rowan & Martin, Butch Cassidy and the Sundance Kid, Robert Redford, and Paul Newman; bell bottoms, halter tops, ten speeds, and microwave ovens. As we settled into what was mod, what was in and what was out, my father landed himself in the hospital again. This time his saviour would be my brother Ken.

When Ken was fourteen and in grade nine he quit school. My parents were dumb-founded because Ken was a very bright boy. His personality was charismatic, all the teachers liked him, and all the girls loved him. Ken was popular and always smiling, standing six feet tall with blonde hair and blue eyes, not the image of our father but certainly holding a similar, contagious sense of humour and personality. Our father, having only a grade seven education, was not too disturbed by Ken's recent decision to quit school, but our mother, of course, wanted her children to succeed academically. She too had not graduated and was hoping that her children would reach that goal. They made one stipulation to Ken, and that was, if he decided to quit school then he must get a job.

KEN GOT A JOB WORKING FOR OUR DAD'S BULLDOZING COMPANY. A chip off the ole block, getting up early and going to work to learn all the ropes of the heavy-duty equipment business. Our father was notably the best Cat operator most people (in the business) had ever seen. We (as a family) had been told this many times by people in the community, and by our mother, and now even Ken would exclaim how talented our dad was. Vince Bonner could eyeball and survey any lot and every job that needed doing with a natural eye and finesse. His estimates of time, measurement, and cost were always right on and the only problem that he ever ran into was under bidding for the sake of the customer, and occasionally having to deal with a few "jokers" (not meant as a nice term) who would not keep up their end of the bargain, sometimes ripping him off because of his down to earth good-natured ways.

An example of this was when my dad lent a neighbor his power saw, and it came back months later, completely dismantled in a million pieces. My father thanked the neighbour for returning it and only complained to our mother what a son of a bitch the guy was, "a real joker," ranted my father.

Seeing her husband's generosity early in the marriage, Frances took it upon herself to be the bad cop of the good cop—bad cop business relationship she had married into. One of my father's favourite stories was when a bill had not been paid by one of his long-standing customers. My mother packed up all three kids in the car (very pregnant with me, her fourth child) and drove over to the man's house to collect the money. When the fellow, the negligent customer, opened his front door, my mother stated, "You need to pay your bill as these children that stand before you need to eat." She received a check for the unpaid bill right then and there.

TRAGEDY AND ANOTHER TEST OF MY FATHER'S WILL TO SURVIVE came at a time when work was slow. My dad was semi-retired, and he was doing some work on the property that he and my mother had purchased four or five years earlier. Together, Ken and my dad were bulldozing and clearing some land on the fifty-acre parcel. After trees had been cut and pushed together, they needed to be burned. On this occasion, when my father poured paint thinners on the fire (how they started fires back then) something caught his attention and as he looked away for a moment, the fumes of the paint thinners rose. When he turned back to the task, with lit match in hand, the air around him combusted into a whoosh of flames. My dad's face, arms, hair and even inside of his throat (as he gasped in flames from the shock of it all) were engulfed in a putrid chemical blaze. He was literally on fire and burning to death. Ken standing nearby started to put the fire on my dad's hair out with his work gloves. Running to find an old blanket, Ken wrapped my dad in the blanket and gave him a few shots of whisky to somehow ease the pain. Not knowing how to drive, but needing to think fast, Ken threw our dad in the passenger side of the pickup truck and managed to drive immediately to the hospital. There was no time or even access to 911 out in the deserted bush in Mission. The hospital was a twenty-minute drive away and the longest twenty minutes for this father and son team that they had ever endured, or would ever have to encounter again.

With third degree burns on his arms, chest, face, and throat Vince Bonner had once again defeated the Grim Reaper.

His recovery was long and arduous. He spent three months in the intensive care unit (again) like before when he had his heart attack, but this time in a different hospital. Mission Memorial hospital was a one-hour drive from North Vancouver where Frances was holding down the fort, a one-hour drive from the comforts of the family home with its green shag carpeting, hi-fi stereo, and orange floral wallpaper in the kitchen, and a one-hour drive from the people he loved. With Linda living in the Interior of British Columbia, Doug finishing high school, and me barely scraping through Grade Five with a C average and too many daydreams, it was Ken who was there for our dad, staying on the property and visiting the hospital daily. My brother would grow up fast, making some mistakes along the way, but loving our family, and to this day feeling like he had the best childhood ever.

My parents thought that the sight of my father covered in bandages, blistering burns underneath, would frighten me. Not seeing my dad during this traumatic time only kept the reality of my father's condition far from my understanding, knowing full well that he was invincible just like superman or batman or a cat with nine lives.

Lions Gate Hospital in North Vancouver

Vince's pride and joy

*Early Lynn Canyon
Suspension Bridge,
North Vancouver*

*Early Cleveland
Dam,
North Vancouver*

CHAPTER 14

Politics and Perfume

My mother told me once that she used to prop us up on the couch when we were babies, with a baby bottle and a few pillows to hold the bottle in place. She gave me this bit of information in a nonchalant way, so matter of fact that I did not take into consideration that we, myself and three siblings, were not held as babies. When I was five years old I had fallen ill with influenza. Too weak to get out of my bed, my mother once and only once, picked me up to rock me in the rocking chair. I remember her gesture as being foreign to me, and I did not know how to sit on her lap or what to do, wondering if I should lean in to her chest, or sit upright away from her. I recall it to be an odd feeling, but happy to be sitting there just the same. She rocked me and sang, that one time. She sang *They Call Me Mellow Yellow*, by Donovan.

It was around this time that my mother came upon a book by child psychologist Doctor Spock. Unfortunately, my siblings were too far past the baby stage to benefit from this brilliant man's teaching, but perhaps there were still enough formative years left in me for my mother to experiment with what this famous doctor had to say. He was ahead of his time in a lot of ways, even though some professionals notably referred to Doctor Spock as a quack.

Needless to say, his thoughts and beliefs made a lot of sense to my mother, as she herself was not raised affectionately. To change how she was brought up was impossible. To change how she parented was somewhat daunting but fortunately because of my father's carefree, fun-loving attitude towards children, both of my parents together as a team complimented one another and did a pretty good job with or without Doctor Spock's views and advice.

Doctor Benjamin McLane Spock 1903-1998 was the first pediatrician to study psychoanalysis to try to understand children's needs and family dynamic. His ideas about childcare influenced several generations to be more flexible and affectionate with their children, and to treat them as individuals. Doctor Spock's book, Baby and Childcare (1946) is one of the best sellers of all time. The book's premise to mothers is that "you know more than you think you do."

Spock went on to write numerous books such as, A Baby's First Year, Dr. Spock Talks with Mothers, Problems of Parents, Caring for Your Disabled Child, A Teenagers Guide to Life and Love, to name a few. His wife, Jane Cheney Spock, assisted in his writing. She was also a civil liberties advocate and mother to their two sons. They divorced in 1974 and Jane then organized and ran support groups for older divorced women.

Spock remarried in 1976 and with his new wife Mary Morgan (forty years his junior) was arrested many times for civil disobedience. Morgan introduced Spock to yoga, massage, meditation, and a macrobiotic diet. Spock wore suits and ties until he was seventy-five years old. Mary Morgan got him to wear his first pair of blue jeans at the age of seventy-five.

When Spock was twenty-one he won a gold medal at the 1924 Olympic Games in Paris, as part of the Olympic rowing crew. At the age of eighty-four, Spock won third place in a rowing contest in Connecticut.

In 1992 Spock received the Peace Abby Courage of
Conscience Award at the John F Kennedy Presidential Library
for his lifelong commitment to disarmament and peaceable
child-rearing. [36]

My mother was also an advocate for various worthy causes
and encouraged my brother Doug in his political thoughts and
views. As a teenager he would go out to picket at the court house,
looking cooler than ever with his long dark hair flowing over his
fringed brown suede jacket. He often rode his ten-speed bicycle,
but my mother usually offered to drive him to his marches and
political activist events, as they were over the Lions Gate Bridge
in Downtown Vancouver.

With Pierre Elliot Trudeau in power as the 15th Prime Minister
of Canada from 1968-1979, 1980-1984 and Nixon winning the
presidential election as the 37th President in the United States
from 1969-1974 there always seemed to be a hotbed of controversy.
There was a lot of conversation in our home that eventually (to my
mother's delight) was summed up quite nicely by *Mad Magazine* and
the TV show *Laugh-In*, records of Nixon calling Trudeau an egg
head and a son of a bitch even though Trudeau supported Nixon
with a phone call during the Watergate investigation.

My favourite part of the magazine was the back cover, which
when laid flat was a cartoon picture of the red haired, freckled boy
with big ears, but when folded into thirds, it turned into something else—a different, controversial cartoon, something I never
could quite understand. My brother found it funny, so naturally
I did too. As kids, not really understanding or knowing what we
were saying, we would traipse all over the neighbourhood quoting
the popular show and its many phrases. My favourite part of the
show was when Goldie Hawn did her go-go dancing in a bikini
and Lily Tomlin played Edith Ann as she sat in a giant oversized
rocking chair, talking like a baby girl. Eventually the show went

off the air. Rumour has it that the show was just too controversial and upsetting.

Mad magazine is an American humour magazine founded in 1952 by Editor Harvey Kurtzman and publisher William Gaines, launched as a comic book before it became a magazine. Based out of Manhattan and then later Madison Avenue, the magazine offered satire on all aspects of life and popular culture, primarily on Politics, entertainment and public figures. [37]

Rowan and Martin's Laugh-in was an American sketch comedy television program that ran for 140 episodes from 1968-1973. The title of the show was a play on the "love-ins" or "be-ins" of the 1960's hippie culture, terms that were derived from sit-ins, common in protests associated with civil rights and anti-war demonstrations of the 60s and early 70s.

Described as a modern-day vaudeville or burlesque show of rapid-fire sketches, comedy routines, and gags, many of which conveyed sexual innuendo or were politically charged. Popular catch phrases such as "Look that up in your Funk and Wagnells" were meant to poke fun at the network's censors. "You bet your sweet bippy," "Beautiful downtown Burbank," "One ringy dingy.... two ring-dingy...." "A gracious and good afternoon. This is Miss Tomlin of the telephone company. Have I reached the party to whom I am speaking with?" "Blow in my ear and I'll follow you anywhere," "Sock it to me," "Here come da judge," "Verrry Interesting," "Well, I'll drink to that," "I did not know that," " You just rang my Chimes." [38]

Occasionally my mother wore Elizabeth Arden perfume and face powder. Very rarely a waft of this powdery scent would pass by me and it brought me comfort and a sense of happiness. I so wanted my mother to be glamorous. She wore knee length, floral house dresses while she did housework. They always had a convenient zipper up the front and places for wadded up tissue in one or both pockets. Her hair was wavy from sponge rollers and she never wore jewellery except her wedding ring and a brooch she won in a bridge tournament. When going out in the community, getting groceries, going to the bank, a night of bridge, or a trip to the bingo parlour, she applied a light dusting of Elizabeth Arden face powder, rouge, and lipstick. It was on these occasions that I thought my mother was pretty but not in a glamorous way like Debbie Reynolds or Doris Day. And when she followed the latest trend of wearing a wig, I loved it when she would let me wear it too. We took turns!

> Elizabeth Arden, with her birth name Florence Nightingale Graham, was a Canadian born, American Business women. Born 1878 – 1966. Elizabeth Arden, Inc. was the cosmetics empire she built in the United States and by 1929 she owned 150 upscale salons across the United States and Europe. In her salons and through her marketing campaigns, Elizabeth Arden stressed teaching women how to apply makeup, and began the concept of beauty makeovers, and coordinating colours of eye, lip and facial makeup. She was the sole owner of her company, and at the peak of her career was one of the wealthiest women in the world. [39]

Once when I had a babysitting job at the age of eleven I asked the parents of the child I was to look after, if I could bring my best friend Mary along with me. They said no. This response greatly disappointed me. Mary in return said, "Well, what if you brought your grandmother to the babysitting job?" Quickly clueing in, we both took to getting her costume ready. My mother's curly brown wig, one of her house dresses, and a few pillows did just the trick, tying Grandma Mary's outfit together with one of my father's belts

and as a magician would say," VOILA!" Mary had been trans-
formed into my make-shift grandmother and off we went to my
babysitting job. She could do an astounding grandmotherly voice
and the child that I was looking after had no idea that Mary was my
eleven-year-old friend and not really my grandmother. However,
I became suspicious when I was not asked back to babysit for this
family again. Perhaps Mary's acting was not as convincing as we
both thought. Not dismayed to have lost my babysitting clients,
I promptly placed the wig back on the Styrofoam fake head until my
mother's next unruly hair day or my need to be someone I was not.

BEING THE YOUNGEST CHILD IN MY FAMILY, WHILE THE OTHERS
were off at school, I naturally spent time with my mother, not
talking or being taught life lessons or skills, but just passing many
a moon being next to her. As I became older I took it upon myself
to partake in charitable deeds. I so wanted to please and to make
just about everyone happy. Was it because of my nick name Smiley?
Or perhaps my giving nature was passed down from both of my
parents and their gentle style of parenting. Was I just seeking
attention to fill my heart that was longing for praise?

When I was snooping in my mother and father's room one day,
in a drawer I found a collection of assorted perfumes, colognes,
and scents that belonged to my mother. Various glass bottles of
different shapes and sizes, never before smelled or even seen by me.
Knowing full well that Elizabeth Arden was my mother's favourite
and chosen perfume, I collected up all the other fragrances, put
them in a brown paper bag and set out delivering them to each of
our neighbours, leaving behind her most treasured, and rarely
worn, Elizabeth Arden. I went door to door, offering my wares
as gifts, as tokens of my love, smiling with pride as each recipient
smiled back at me. My Mother never got mad or annoyed. She

simply suggested that I ask for permission next time. And that was that.

Colouring and making pictures for the bridge club was another one of my favourite pastimes. Wanting to please, I would sit at the kitchen table for hours, painstakingly ripping pages out of my most recent colouring book, ensuring that I had enough for everyone that would come to our home for a game of cards. Before the bridge club arrived, I went around with my mother, setting up tables and chairs, allocating one ash tray per table and putting out mixed nuts, Liquorice Allsorts and mints, creating the perfect ambiance for each guest. I would spend my time before bed with my waxy Crayola crayons, trying to stay in the lines to create perfect works of art for each visitor. I abruptly stopped doing this the day after I heard my mother complain to my father how disrespectful she thought it was when some of the ladies left behind my colouring gift and how she hid the abandoned keepsakes, so my feelings would not be hurt. I felt bad that my mother felt bad.

OH, HOW I WANTED TO BE A TEACHER, TO STAND IN FRONT OF A classroom of students, teaching, demonstrating, and handing out assignments. Marking the completed work afterwards would be the best part of all. That's when the idea of playing school with the younger neighbourhood children came to fruition.

The long drawn out days of summer brought with them boredom. When not going to work with my father, Ambleside beach with my mother, swimming lessons at the North Shore Winter Club, camping trips or hide and seek at night, we would play school. I found an old cow bell that worked as a school bell (Little House on the Prairie style!) and in our basement where my mother ironed and watched her soap operas we had a big old oak desk (from the bank my older sister Linda worked at) perfect for the teacher, meaning me. I used my earnings from babysitting to purchase work books at London Drugs and my father had done some bulldozing work for the school board, so they gave him seven small primary desks. Just right for my students. I taught math, grammar, hand writing, and science. The parents of the neighbourhood children who attended my school were none other than thrilled. I received gifts of appreciation regularly, from a five-dollar bill to a big ole salmon that one of the dads had caught. We had recess, homework, and field trips. Once my dad piled us all into the back of his pickup truck for a field trip to the park. Sitting on the floor with our backs up against the cab, jostling around, long before it was illegal to have human bodies strewn about in the back of a pick-up truck.

Doug at the school newspaper, looking cool, Sutherland High School

Handsome Ken

CHAPTER 15

Barbie Dolls and Boyfriends

In March 1959 the first Barbie Doll was launched by the American toy company, Mattel, Inc. American Business woman Ruth Handler, the co-founder of Mattel, copied a German prostitute doll called Bild Lilli as her inspiration. Barbie's job was to serve as a teenage fashion doll. Her full name was Barbara Millicent Roberts and she appeared in a series of novels published by Random House in the 1960s. Skipper Roberts was created in 1964 as Barbie's little sister. The intention behind the development of Skipper was to oppose controversies directed at Barbie for being too sexual in appearance as the first doll ever to have breasts. [40]

MY FIRST BARBIE DOLL WAS A SKIPPER DOLL THAT WAS GIVEN TO me for my fifth birthday. My second Barbie Doll was a black doll named Juliet, a single mom who worked as a nurse. She came in the package, wearing a nurse outfit with an attached, Going Out at Night, sparkly disco pantsuit. Later I received a traditional Barbie, followed by Ken, a Barbie house, car and camper. Ken and Barbie were married so one needed a wedding dress, in addition to many other outfits. Malibu Barbie was my favourite. She came with a permanent suntan, a twist and turn waist, wearing a light blue one-piece bathing suit and sunglasses holding back her beautiful shiny long blonde hair. Barbie and Ken did not work, they just zoomed around in their convertible. Sometimes they would take Skipper, but she had to lay down on the top of the trunk as there was not enough room. They loved to camp and sleep in Kleenex boxes. Sometimes they would all go swimming in the bath tub, but the water and bubbles usually ruined their hair. (Not Ken's because his hair was plastic and moulded to his head!!)

AS FAR BACK AS I CAN REMEMBER, MY GRANDPA JOE LIVED WITH us. That is until the day he left to move back in with my grandmother. My grandmother lived with my Auntie Violet in Vernon. Every day of his life, my grandfather wore a three-piece suit with a tie, fancy shoes like Fred Astaire, and a hat on top of his bald head. Without exception, he had a cloth handkerchief in his top right-hand pocket. He would take it out from time to time to polish his head or blow his nose. Inside his suit jacket he kept a great big watch on a long chain, looking like a bona fide, dapper gentleman. His bedroom was tidy and mysterious, containing a small bed, desk, chair, and a Bible that he scribbled notes in. There was also a cross with that religious man hanging from it. I found out much later that it was Jesus. They killed him because he said he was the Son of God. They did not believe him, so they took nails and hammered him up on a gigantic cross. He seemed like such a nice man, I often thought.

Grandpa Joe told my mother that he thought we, my brothers, sister, and myself were spoiled. We had bicycles, televisions, swimming lessons, and many toys, from hot wheels to my bedroom full of Barbie dolls. He said we ran around the neighbourhood like chickens with our heads cut off! I had never seen a chicken with its head cut off and I surely did not want to. Mary told me that they really do run around without a head if it happens to get cut off.

At eight years old this information was hard to understand, as I liked running around the neighbourhood playing Cops and Robbers and Cowboys and Indians. At night time there was Hide and Seek, and sometimes my older brothers would play Soldier and they would let me be the nurse. For some reason though, they never got injured so I would wait endlessly in my play house, which was also the medic station, but no one ever came for me to bandage them up.

Aside from his remark about us being spoiled, Grandpa Joe loved children. He would clap at my cartwheels, and with his thick French-Canadian accent he would exclaim, "again, again, again", just like a child at the circus wanting the clowns to do another trick.

Every day Grandpa would write a letter to his wife, my grandmother. Sitting at his little desk in his bedroom, he would call me in, and even if I had a friend over, they too would get called in to see my grandpa. With letter in hand he would ask us to take it to the mailbox on the corner. Off we would go, on a mission to do a small job for Grandpa Joe. In appreciation, he would give my friend twenty-five cents and I would get a mint. And then feeling badly, he would give my friend a mint too!

WHEN I WAS IN GRADE SIX, AFTER MY DAD HAD RECOVERED FROM his heart attack, we all went on a trip to Hawaii. My sister had long since moved away, so she did not join us. Linda lived up north and she was an honest to goodness cowgirl, with horses, rodeos, cowboys, cowboy boots, and hats. Everyone up there hunted for moose to keep in their freezer through the winter. We visited her sometimes and it was fun to be the little sister of a cowgirl. We rode horses at the Big Bar Ranch.

After finding out about the Hawaiian vacation, my teacher
suggested that I keep a scrapbook and a journal to record my trip.
This would be a school assignment as well as a nice keepsake that
I could show my own children someday, he said. I started writing
in my journal from the minute we got on the plane, a Boeing 747.

> Boeing's most famous plane, the 747 is an American wide-
> body commercial jet airliner and cargo aircraft.
> Often referred to as The Jumbo Jet, it was first flown on
> February 9, 1969 and then commercially flown in 1970. It sold
> at a list price of twenty-four million dollars. It had a partial
> double deck and a spiral staircase upstairs to a lounge area
> and additional seating. There are roughly nine hundred 747s
> left today. [41]

The best part about being on an airplane were the stewardesses.
They were like real human Barbie Dolls whose job was to travel
in an airplane and bring people their food and blankets millions
of miles up in the sky. Our meals were delivered with a sweet,
sing-song lilt and came on tiny china dishes— a salad, roll, main
course, tea and dessert, compact and segmented. I always liked the
saying "coffee, tea, or me?!"
A stewardess was like a model, waitress, and nurse rolled into
one women. She got to wear a tight little suit jacket and fitted
skirts, high heels, and a tiny little hat perched on beautiful coiffed
hair. It was love at first sight; I decided from that moment on that
I too wanted to be an airline stewardess when I grew up—the most
glamorous job in the world.
The worst part of being transported in the sky was the thick
layer of cigarette smoke that loomed over our heads. It slowly
crept down from the overhead baggage compartment to engulf us,
hindering our breathing, sinus pathways, and lungs as the plane
propelled us forward. My ears hurt like the dickens and the air

was hot, and unbearably stuffy. How those stewardesses stayed so fresh and friendly, I'll never know. But one day I would learn their secrets, and I would become one of them, providing my nightly prayers were answered that I would become pretty. Pretty and thin with big boobs was the main goal in nightly prayers to the little dead man on my grandfather's cross, hanging above his bedroom door.

Once we landed, we said goodbye to our caregivers above the clouds, and were greeted by beautiful Hawaiian ladies who adorned us with flower necklaces that we learned were called Leis. They smelled like Heaven and they gave our noses a nice cleansing from the stagnant cigarette smoke and other people's breathing.

Much to my dismay, we had to board another airplane to take us just a little bit further to the Island of Maui. Once there, we were all cranky, tired, and bothered. Arriving at the condominium complex that would be our home for the next two weeks, we found that we could not check in for another three hours.

Both of my teenage brothers' eyes started rolling, while I whined about the heat and glaring sunshine. My mother had the bright idea of us all changing into our swimsuits to swim in the pool until it was time to check in. Out came her book and we all easily settled into some fun in the sun.

Raised poor, and now working class, with my mother's sights set on becoming middle class, my father decided to roam around the grounds to check out our new surroundings. My dad always recommended that I peruse the lay of the land wherever I happened to be. "Get to know where the exits are and be ready to plan your route of escape," he would frequently instruct. He proceeded to do this while we all frolicked out of harm's way at the pool.

Admiring the gardens and how sturdy the front porches were built at each unit, my father eventually stumbled upon the resort's caretaker. Striking up a conversation, he offered a nice firm hand shake, and his usual introduction of, "Hi, I'm Vince Bonner of Vince Bonner Bulldozing from North Vancouver, British

Columbia, Canada." We, his four children often scoffed at his big introduction, with smirks of laughter or unbridled embarrassment. However, it was his schtick and it always worked. The maintenance man took an immediate shining to my dad. He loved that we were from Canada and he explained to my father how the rich Americans came in and bought up all the beach front property, forcing his family and many others to build their homes in the jungle.

Without taking a breath, his second sentence was, "Here, take the keys to my car and go get supplies for you and your family". My father was initially flabbergasted at the stranger's generous, trusting offer. Without batting an eye, my father went and got my mother, and together they took the groundskeeper's car and headed to the nearest grocery store.

My brothers and I stayed in the pool awaiting our check-in and the Luau, which was a Hawaiian dinner party consisting of Huli-Huli Pineapple chicken, Spicy Teriyaki Spam, Maui-Maui Ribs, Hawaiian Chicken Kabobs, and coconut drinks with fancy straws and tiny umbrellas. The best part of the evening would be the Hawaiian floor show. There were fire dancers, hula girls, and people invited up from the audience to put on a grass skirt and two coconuts for a bra! This had us all in stitches, laughing at the hapless volunteers from the crowd learning the Hula Dance.

Our new local Hawaiian friend would eventually introduce us to his beautiful family, and take my father deep into the jungle to pick his own coconuts. He was a lovely man, hospitable and kind, and our new family friend. This vacation to Hawaii came with so many memories for me and my family; memories of pineapple groves, sugar cane factories, beaches and coral, Hula dancers, and whales in the sea.

All of this was recorded in my journal. Glued in with the pages were tropical scenic post cards, drawings, and samples of sugar cane. I documented the history of the Hawaiian Islands from the local maintenance man's point of view and included my thoughts on travel and the different people that we met. There were even stories about girls both of my brothers dated during the short term of our vacation. I was bursting with pride and excitement to show my teacher when I returned!

The day we arrived home it was snowing. My father grabbed the Kodak instamatic camera to take my photograph. I was dressed in my sandals, floral muumuu, and flower petal lei. He took the photo of me, suntan and all, standing in two inches of snow. Thank goodness there was a flash cube!

On the first day back to school, I proudly handed over my masterpiece, my work of art. The teacher, with a wink and a nod, took my showpiece and shoved it in his briefcase, only for me to never see it again! So long to my treasured assignment and memories of an unforgettable family vacation in Hawaii; my teacher never returned my project to me.

BEFORE I KNEW IT, I WAS ON TO GRADE EIGHT. GOODBYE TO THE childish days of elementary school with field trips, hot dog days, and spelling tests.

"Being a teenager is like having a mental illness." I read that in a book somewhere, a self-help book that taught parents how to cope with a teenager. Life as a teenager is by no means easy. Even though adults deal with everything from work problems to debt, no period of your life comes close to being as difficult as your teenage years.

YOUR BODY, MIND, AND THOUGHT PROCESSES, BOTH PHYSICAL and emotional, are changing as you are thrust into some of the most intense situations of your young life, discovering heartbreak, anxiety, low self-esteem, and peer pressure along the way. With expectations both academically and socially, combined with hormones and puberty, life as you once knew it drastically changes. Science has proven the mood swings and erratic behaviour is all part of growing up. Teenagers are not awkward and confrontational by choice, which creates an emotional roller coaster ride for everyone involved. Independence and privacy, disagreements with parents, figuring out your identity, proms, drinking and drugs, sex and love, and often bullying, are all happening while you are trying to figure out what you want to be when you grow up.

How much responsibility is given to young people depends on the parents and their method of parenting, how they were raised, and their own stress level or shortcomings, perhaps not knowing how to cope or what to do with a disagreeable child. Discipline in all forms is used, strategized, and experimented with—spankings, the strap, time outs, ultimatums, bribery, or harsh words meant to improve us or change us or get through our thick skull that something is wrong with us.

As parents we continuously strive to give our children a better life, a life more full, a path less bumpy than we ourselves had. We want an upbringing with more opportunities, open-mindedness, less stress and oppression than perhaps we were shown. Who's to say what "better" means? Is it better to talk things out rather than to discipline? Is it better to give choices—would you like to do this, or would you like to do that? And at what age do we instill the importance of decision making? Or when do we begin to give out responsibility? Two years of age? Four years of age? Six, or perhaps twelve? What happens if the parents come from a dysfunctional family themselves and they were never taught or shown how to be an effective parent?

When I was twelve, going on thirteen, my parents sat me down and asked me the unforgettable question—would I like to move out to the farm? Pack up everything, lock, stock, and barrel, and leave all I had ever known, and North Vancouver, the beloved city of my birth? The farm of course, being the fifty acres of land that my parents had purchased six years prior, which consisted of a log cabin, three trout ponds, a barn, a horse, horse trails, and a neighbourhood school bus for pick up and drop off. No words or scenarios went along with this question, such as: if we move, you will have to make all new friends; if we relocate to Stave Falls, the high school, stores, town, and community will be a twenty-minute drive (each way) on rural winding roads; if we move you will spend a lot of time alone and if you want to participate in after school activities (meaning a basketball game or an occasional school dance), WE, your dorky parents, will have to drive you. If any of these details had been presented to me, if there had been a master plan or a synopsis, I wonder if my decision would have been different.

STARTING GRADE NINE AND A NEW AND IMPROVED LIFE WAS JUST a hopeful thought away. My thinking at the time was that perhaps if I moved, I might be more popular at my new school. Maybe my grades would get better and just maybe I would become thinner, prettier, and less shy. Owning a horse was definitely a selling feature. And I did always love going to the farm on the weekends with my dad and my best friend Mary. So, without a blink of an eye or a day to ponder, I said," Yes, I want to move." And just like that, based on Karen's quick, thoughtless answer, the packing began.

Late one evening, before we moved from our cosy little neighbourhood, the dream home that my parents built in 1946, I heard some unrecognisable sounds coming from the kitchen. It sounded like crying. I was sitting in my room with my favourite cat Ginger, the stray cat that wandered into my life seven years previous; the cat that I told all my secrets to in whispered moments under my covers; the cat that would gaze warmly into my eyes when I wished I could transform myself into her, yearning that instead of going to school or to the dentist, I could become a cat and all my problems would go away. I would curl into a ball and sleep the day away or maybe watch soap operas with my mother. To be a cat would free me of all responsibilities.

It was on this night I realised that perhaps the move to the farm was not a mutual decision. The decision was possibly too much responsibility for a shy, twelve-year-old girl with rail road track braces, a pre-teen who still played with Barbie Dolls and desperately wanted to be grown up enough to have a boyfriend.

When I crept out of my bedroom to see where the noise was coming from, I spied my mother sobbing at the kitchen table, with the orange floral table cloth still holding the bowl of saltines and crumbs strewn about from that night's dinner of pot roast. The table now supported my mother's head as she hunched over it, shoulders shaking, her body heaving with quiet deep sobs. My father hovered over her with a look of helplessness and despair written on his face, engulfing his whole body, turning him into a smaller version of himself. Before I could even grasp what was going on, I flew back to my bedroom, quietly shutting my door and burying my head under the pink ballerina bed spread, while Ginger looked on. Safely in the confines of my own room, where I had often imagined a better life, the uncomfortable scene that I had just witnessed was foreign to me. Even though I had cried frequently, or so it seemed, never before had I seen my mother cry. Never. There I sat on my perfectly made bed thinking of how I had carelessly and thoughtlessly changed the course of my family's life. I was now experiencing my mother's pain and my father's despair for the first time, at the age of twelve, soon to be thirteen. That was a long time to go, with only seeing happiness, or no emotion at all. Seeing what was going on in the kitchen with my parents was new and somehow felt wrong. Why hadn't they said something? Why did they ask me if I wanted to move? And why had I been protected (up until now) from these natural releases of feelings, tears, and despair?

In 1972, looking back on my somewhat short life, I had been sheltered, mentally, emotionally, and spiritually, because when my parents were children they had felt immeasurable pain, crying buckets until there were no more tears to fall. They grew up with their ruddy little faces soggy from weeping silent tears, my father withdrawing into days of daydreaming and fantasizing about a better life, my mother becoming defiant and pledging that she would not cry ever again, determined that her mother would not get the best of her. Both of my parents had lost their natural carefree innocence, repeatedly having their hopes, dreams, and wishes dashed cruelly. There were no choices, or teachings on how to cope, just comments like, "Children should be seen and not heard," and "Stop crying or I will give you something to cry about." They were left shattered and broken, like an irreparable mirror void of reflection, with no comfort or methods of rebuilding their sad little souls.

Both my mom and dad, separately, and with completely different upbringings, said to themselves when they were small, with their weary heads buried in their gentle hands, "When I become a mommy/daddy I will do things differently." They both decided at an early age that their own children would never witness bickering or yelling, that their children would only grow up with positive words and they would say the word yes more than they would say the word no.

As easily as the question was asked about moving, so too was my answer thrown out freely. "Yes, I would love to move," was my response, while the voice in my head said, "Get me out of here and let my life begin!"

I did not know that it would be the beginning of my mother's demise. The coddled life she provided for us, the home baked bread and chocolate cupcakes, would soon lose their lustre. The bridge club, swimming lessons, and afternoon matinees over the bridge would abruptly halt. With no warning my mother would regress into many dark years of depression, void of communication and expression. Ahead were manic states, anger, and bouts of wild humour and reckless financial strain. I would become a self-absorbed teenager, not seeing or noticing the gradual changes in my mother. I was at the stage when a young girl is bubbling over with life, thoughts and forever-changing dreams of an adventurous future, displaying the normal teenage awkwardness, insecurities, and mixed up emotion. But somewhere in the back of my mind I missed the mother I used to have and the community of family that we had in North Vancouver.

The move to Mission went without incident. Movers with their moving trucks, packers with their heavy-duty cardboard boxes and coat hangers pretty much did the entire move. Out with the old and on with the new. Except, instead of moving forward, it was as if we were moving backwards. A two-bedroom, rustic log house, complete with a wood burning stove, septic tank and a well with a sump pump that often went dry over the summer months. My father did his best by adding gold flecked shag carpeting upstairs and linoleum with a rusty brick pattern downstairs. He also purchased some modern furniture from the Sears catalogue—two couches with a wagon wheel, cowboy covered-wagon motif. But that in itself seemed out-dated and somehow forced, because my mother stopped smiling and became void of all expression; she became absent and detached, completely uninvolved in everything. My mother had checked out.

Growing up I was taught to laugh and smile freely and openly, but was sent to my room if there were tears or emotion that was unacceptable. Therefore my mother's new persona was so out of the ordinary that I thought it was better left alone. So, I ignored it.

THE FIRST SUMMER AFTER THE MOVE FLEW PAST WHILE I TOOTLED around the backwoods on my horse Cricket and swam in the above-ground pool. Then, abruptly, the inevitable arrived – September, Grade nine, and my new school.

The bus shack was at least a mile away and to prevent me from being kidnapped or murdered my father would drive me the distance to wait for the school bus. The year before we moved out to our property, there had been a contest for all the rural kids to paint their bus shacks. I never found out who had won the competition, but I guessed that it was not the bus shack that I got dropped off at. Ours was painted light blue with black trim and meagre, hand scrawled cartoons strewn about. A few holes kicked in the side did not seem like a contest winner. Either way, it was shelter from the rain and a place to sit. Although our bus shack was at the end of the line, and we were the last to be picked up, the bus would turn around there and drive back to town. This was convenient for anyone who missed it the first time, because they were still able to catch it the second time. The bus route went through Stave Falls, both coming and going, and then south over the Stave Lake Dam, through Steel Head, and on to Mission High School. We were often referred to as Hill Billies because of where we lived.

My new bus shack friends were Rachael, Jesse, and Kelly. Rachael was one year younger than me with blonde pigtail braids, a red plaid shirt and blue jeans (always), and a love of horses. She was painfully shy, and I liked her immediately. Jesse was seemingly a mean tough boy who only showed up periodically to wait for the bus. Once he had with him a brown paper sack, lunch bag size, saying that it was filled with magic mushrooms. Since I had never heard of magic mushrooms, I did not pay much attention but, somehow, I knew they were not the kind of mushrooms my father would fry up with butter, salt, and pepper. Lastly there was Kelly, very pretty with a hardened country-girl style. She did not say much, but I liked her too, even though we rarely spoke. Rumour had it that her brother had killed someone from the street that I lived on.

Rain or shine, we would sit every morning inside the dank bus shelter, waiting to go to the same place. Along the way the bus would stop to pick up other kids. Sarah who eventually became my best friend, Rosie and her four sisters and two brothers, and Ellen who was Sarah's friend before I was. These girls played an important part in my upcoming teenage years. It was here on the twenty-minute bus ride to school that I would socialize with my new friends, who would help me cope and fit in during a ridiculously awkward time. It was on this daily drive that we would finish up homework, gossip about the crushes we all had, and experience the bullying that always upset us, but forced us to look the other way. Our bus driver Cookie, greeted us with a boisterous "Good morning!" and allowed us to listen to our favourite radio station, 14CFUN. "Stairway to Heaven" was a symbolic song, ushering us into what we considered to be hell on earth. On arriving at school we would disembark from the safety of our cocoon on wheels and escape to different universal groupings.

I invited the school bus friends, whom I called my "at home school friends" to join the Rolly Lake Trail Riders. This was a horseback riding club that my sister initiated, being a cowgirl, and loving anything western. Anyone with a horse could join. However, since not everyone in the neighbourhood had a horse, my sister would lend hers out, so all could participate. It was convenient having my sister heading up our little riding club, because she lived next door. She would store all of the ribbons and trophies from our events right there in her trailer, and we would often have our meetings there.

The intention of my father when he bought the fifty acres of land in 1968 was to sub-divide it into five-acre parcels and divide them between his four children. My sister Linda was the first to get her land. Before we moved to the log cabin that my father and brother built, and after the cabin had burned down and was built back up again, my sister put a mobile home on her plot of land. It was situated near the barn, next to a man-made trout pond just over a scenic foot bridge, all created and built by my father for convenience and practicality. Linda worked for a bank and commuted daily in her pickup truck to her place of employment. In the early mornings and evenings she would tend to the horses. There was Big Dolly and Little Dolly, her horse Jack and my horse Cricket.

After we moved to the cabin, my father did most of the daily work in addition to raising chickens, a cow named Burt, the bull, pigs who had baby piglets, and an occasional sheep or goat. It was a Hobby Farm and my father loved it. For him it became a place of refuge, a place my mother never allowed herself to go.

Trails were created on the property with my dad's bulldozer. Scenes were made to emulate the old west—a man completely dressed in all western attire with cowboy boots and hat, dutifully hanging by the neck from a tree, as well as an old abandoned graveyard called Boot Hill, with graves for the likes of Billy the Kid and Jesse James. All the riding trails meandered and connected through lush old growth forests, with twists and turns along the way. It was not uncommon to spot a deer or a brown bear caught off-guard and then quickly escaping the clamouring horses and chatter from the exuberant trail riders.

Word got around and soon the Rolly Lake Trail Riders were formed. Basically, it was a horseback riding club that had various activities, monthly meetings, and a whole lot of fun for a bunch of kids from the country. A Play Day, like a mini rodeo in our corral on the last Sunday of every month, would have us all participating and competing against each other in Barrel Races or the Sack Race where the rider was to stand inside a burlap sack and hop across the sawdust-laden corral while leading their horse to the finish line. The Rescue Race would have the rider and horse gallop to one end of the corral to pick up another rider, doubling them back to the finish line. Musical Sacks was like musical chairs, leading one's horse around a circle of sacks, and when the music stopped, the rider and horse needed to be near a sack or they would have to leave the game. My sister supplied ribbons and trophies bought with the money from the hotdog stand that my mother operated. High or low with her depression, my mother would dutifully contribute locally brand-named Pop Shop pop and microwaved hot dogs with mustard and ketchup set up outside on a card table. Hotdogs and pop were purchased by the Rolly Lake Trail Riders, friends, family, and neighbours who were attending the Play Day. All proceeds went toward the trophies and ribbons and occasional field trips in my sister's car to the horse auction in Matsqui.

It was during one of the meetings that the gossip buzz zeroed in on the new boy in town. Margaret Dundle had spotted him. Margaret did not have a horse or participate in the Play Days, but she was the secretary to all the meetings. Naturally she had the goods on what was going on in our small community of Stave Falls, a twenty-minute drive east of Maple Ridge and a twenty-minute drive north west of Mission.

During the summer before Grade Nine had started and before the new friends started to appear I had an obsession, or rather a love of a television actor and singer by the name of David Cassidy. It was true love and my heart ached for him. Tuning in every Friday night to the hit show, *The Partridge Family*, I could dream and swoon over TV character Keith Partridge, AKA David Cassidy. I wrote letters, bought teen heartthrob magazines and filled scrap book after scrap book with photographs of the boy I would never meet, never date, and never marry. It was a bittersweet conundrum. I was even jealous of the TV characters who played his girlfriends on the show—doomed right from the get-go!

Eventually I would carry a torch for Vinnie Barbarino from the TV show, *Welcome Back Kotter*, AKA John Travolta, and later, Robert Redford from movies such as *A Star is Born*, *Barefoot in the Park*, *Butch Cassidy and the Sundance Kid*, *The Sting*, and *The Great Gatsby*. All I wanted was a boyfriend, preferably one from the above list, and to live happily ever after.

All my aspirations and longing for love were to be fulfilled by one boy, the mysterious new boy in town who owned two horses and lived a couple of miles down the road. The question—who was going to invite him to be a part of our group, the Rolly Lake Trail Riders? Margaret Dundle elected herself.

Sure enough, at our next horse group meeting, there he was, a combination of Keith Partridge, Vinnie Barbarino, and Robert Redford all rolled into one human being—Todd Barnes. Todd had feathered shoulder length brown hair, wide set, almond shaped, green eyes, and an adorable space between his two front teeth. He was the most handsome boy I had ever met. He even wore two-inch clogs, high-waisted, wide leg, faded blue jeans, and a short brown leather bomber jacket! The best part about meeting Todd and having him be a part of the Rolly Lake Trail Riders was that it was me he wanted.

Flattered, honoured, and desperately wanting a boyfriend, the riding group took on a whole new meaning for me. Rolly Lake Trail Riders was not just a trail riding horse club anymore, but rather a place to see my new boyfriend. Margaret Dundle wanted him too, and she tried her best to snag him, but it was me that Todd began to make eyes at from across the room at every horse club meeting.

Summing up Grade Nine and Ten, I had a new high school, immediate friends, a club to belong to, a horse to take care of, and the prospects of a gorgeous boyfriend. Suddenly my mother isolating herself and hibernating into depression did not matter so much to me.

I was fifteen, inexperienced, awkward, and shy. Todd told me that he was nineteen, quite a bit older than me, but girls mature faster, right? We would soon become boyfriend and girlfriend. I now had a partner at all the Play Day events. Todd would hoist me up behind him for the rescue race and cheer for me from the sidelines for the barrel races. He would come over and watch the Vancouver Canucks play on Hockey Night in Canada. We would listen to records and occasionally go to a movie. Rod Stewart was our favourite singer. For my fifteenth birthday Todd gave me three pairs of the most beautiful earrings I had ever seen. I was dreaming of finishing high school and building castles in the air with Todd Barnes. Mrs. Todd Barnes........I had visualised our apartment, the furniture in it, and inviting my mother over lunch. My life would be better than *The Partridge Family*, more fun than *Welcome Back Kotter* and just as romantic as *The Great Gatsby*!

Then Todd started pressuring me. The phrase I had never heard before, but later learned was a common phrase then and unfortunately now—"If you really love me, no, really love me, you would have sex with me". Breaking and giving in, the whole experience was awful for me. Afterwards, I found out the man of my dreams, Todd Barnes, was really twenty-two years old. I was fifteen.

Soon enough, after nine months of dating, Todd Barnes moved away. Later I found out that his parents had set him up at the property he was staying at to straighten him out. He had caused a fair bit of trouble in Surrey where they lived and they needed someone looking after their horses. Just as quickly as he had arrived, he left, like a thief in the night. I was heartbroken and relieved all at the same time once he was gone.

Frances and Vince, Aloha

Karen home from Hawaii

CHAPTER 16

"Rescuing" Grandma

SHORTLY AFTER WE HAD SETTLED ON THE ACREAGE, MY GRAND-mother phoned my mother and said, "Please come and get me, because Violet is being mean to me." Most daughters, upon hearing such a request, would be on the next bus, plane, train, or vehicle, to retrieve their mother from the clutches of harm's way. This is what we set out to do.

My mother and father, my brother Ken and his girlfriend, and thirteen-year-old me all piled into our bright yellow custom 500 Ford and headed to Vernon where Auntie Violet and my grand-mother lived. This road trip with my family felt like the beginning of an epic adventure. It was an exciting and mysterious journey, a rescue mission to bring my grandmother safely home to live with us.

Leaving bright and early for the retrieval, we listened to a Gordon Lightfoot eight track tape (repeatedly) along the way, until my older brother said that he would truly be Alberta Bound if he had to listen to one more song. Personally, I loved the woeful churning of Lightfoot's ballads, visualizing myself as a Damsel in Distress aboard the "Edmund Fitzgerald", a once popular radio-worthy song by the famous Canadian singer.

As we drove out of the Fraser Valley and through the township of Hope, my father told the story of the Hope slide as we entered the Hope-Princeton Highway.

> The Hope slide was the second largest landslide ever recorded in Canada. It happened on January 9th 1965 in the Nicolum Valley in the Cascade Mountains, near Hope, British Columbia, on a stretch of the Hope-Princeton Highway below Johnson Peak. Prior to the landslide, a small avalanche had forced five people to stop a few miles south-east of the town of Hope. However, two earthquakes had occurred, causing the slide to obliterate the mountain's southwestern slope. Buried in the slide was a hay truck with its driver, a yellow convertible, and an Oil Tanker. Prior to being buried, Oil Truck driver Norman Stephanishin had stopped behind the convertible, who had stopped because the road was blocked. Norman suggested they all turn around and head back to Sumallo Lodge. The driver of the car and the hay truck refused to join him so Norman, who was unable to turn his Oil truck around, decided to walk 4 km to the Lodge. On his trek he flagged down a bus and convinced the driver to back up and go no further. [42]

As my father told the story, the bus backed up in the nick of time, as earth, rocks, and boulders came crashing down in a second slide, in the exact area the bus was about to travel through. The driver of the bus, David Hughes, is credited for saving the passengers of the bus, including Norman. Unfortunately, those who had stayed behind perished, two of the bodies never to be found.

As we now drove past the remaining devastation, seven years after the incident, my father told the story in a serious, respectful tone. I felt saddened but fascinated with my dad's recollection and his way with words. As we wound through boulders the size of Volkswagen bugs, it seemed unreal to me that people had died there.

Approaching Princeton, we began to devise a plan for Grandma's escape. On the telephone to my mother, Grandma had stated that Violet must not know that we were coming. It would have to look like a casual visit that would somehow turn into a kidnapping!

Plan A

My mother and father were to meet Auntie Violet and my grandmother in a local coffee shop, while my brother, his girlfriend, and I were to drive to the mobile home, take my grandmother's medication and a few articles of clothing, and head back to the coffee shop. We would park outside and wait for our parents to emerge with my grandmother, and off we would go. My grandma would be free and we would merrily go back to our home in Mission.

Plan B

There was no plan B. So off we went.

Dropping my parents off at the coffee shop in Vernon, with seventeen-year-old Ken behind the wheel, we raced out to Grandma and Auntie Violet's trailer. Once inside the trailer there was an eerie feel, almost like a staged crime. Photo albums had been strewn about the spotlessly clean living room. Pages had been ripped out, photographs had been cut to shreds, and the scissors still remained on the kitchen table.

Hurriedly we went about our business. My brother grabbed an armload of Grandma's clothes and I took the pills from the medicine cabinet. We ran back out to the car and screeched off. Just as we were leaving the confines of the park gates, who did we pass coming the other way, but a police car, sirens wailing, and a clear visual of Auntie Violet in the back seat, instructing the officer where to go!

Later we put the pieces together. Somehow Grandma had divulged our plan to Auntie Violet, and she was hoping to catch us in the act of burglary. Fortunately we got away, just like an episode of *The Rockford Files* with James Garner. After reaching the restaurant, we excitedly picked up our parents and grandma to begin the trip back. My dad later told us the story of how Auntie Violet had caused quite a scene in the restaurant. She had picked up a coffee cup to strike my father, exclaiming for all to hear that my dad was actually her husband, and how dare he bring his floozy (my mother) to town! My father had to once again restrain my aunt as my mother froze in the booth not knowing what to do. It was shortly after the outlandish dramatics that Auntie Violet fled the restaurant, flagging down a police car to attempt a sneak attack upon us while we were still in her trailer.

Six hours later we were at home making up a bed in my grandmother's new bedroom.

Grandma only lasted with us for three weeks. Unfortunately, in my thirteen-year-old haste, I failed to look at the name on the prescription bottle when I stole Grandma's pills. I had accidentally taken the cat's medicine. So Grandma was without her pills, the cat was without its pills, and Auntie Violet had somehow changed. She had started calling daily, begging Grandma to return.

What could we do? Grandma was driven to Abbotsford and placed on a bus back to Vernon and into the seemingly loving arms of her eldest daughter, who without a doubt needed her mother.

The kitty lived on.

The Hope slide, Hope British Columbia

Ken & Karen on route to rescue Grandma

CHAPTER 17

Shop Lifting and Beauty Pageants

OVER THE YEARS MY MOTHER WOULD COME IN AND OUT OF HER depression and even though she was not there for me during my first boyfriend debacle, being deeply tied up in her own misery, she was more than happy when Todd moved away. Perhaps this was the shift that she needed. Life would continue and my mother would be back on top for a time.

She tried joining a bowling league and started volunteering with the Meals on Wheels program. She didn't last long at her charity job because she kept getting lost. Always a nervous driver and not a map reader, she was not able to find the addresses where she needed to deliver the meals. Mom would show up late with cold food. Plus, she said the old people on the receiving end depressed her.

At night my mom, dad, and I would sit down to dinner and then tune in to watch *Three's Company*, *Laverne and Shirley*, and our all-time favourite television show, *Happy Days*. We would all chuckle at Jack Tripper, trying to live with two female roommates, in love with both of them and yet dating others. The mischief and jams Laverne and Shirley would get into! And of course, there was Arthur Fonzarelli, "The Fonz", whom we all loved. Life was a half hour sitcom, then we would go to bed, getting up the next day to repeat it all over again.

My father would drive me to the school bus shack, bring my mother breakfast in bed, and then putter around our property while I was attending high school, manoeuvring my way around friendships, crushes on boys, and school work that I barely understood.

In between my mother's low days, she would have high days. This could be comforting and fun, like when she would buy a whole new wardrobe, or make plans for us to travel. It was just me still at home so the three of us would pack up in the middle of the school year and just go. My parents would allow me to pick out the accommodations from the travel brochure, so once again, if the place sucked it was because I had chosen it. However, more times than not, the places where we stayed were fine, three-star hotels that met my country girl standards.

In Grade Eleven my parents took me and my friend Sarah to Hawaii. This was an amazing trip for both of us. Two weeks of surf, sun, Pooka shells and tank tops. We took surfing lessons and worked on our tans.

Another pastime on my mother's high days were her outlandish, over-the-top ideas that were so extreme they were simply not do-able. Letters to the President of the United States, a tell-all book never to be finished, called *Don't Tell Daddy*, or bags and bags of half-knitted sweaters. Her worst idea of all was to open a Bed and Breakfast. It was these manic ideas that exhausted my father, irritated everyone around her and made all of us in the family unsure of what to do with her.

Sometimes her manic behaviour was tolerable and even comical, like the time she sent my grad photo to the producers of her favourite soap opera, *The Young and the Restless,* asking them if they could put me on the series, claiming I was beautiful and "just right for the part!"

Once, when we were on vacation in Mexico, she purchased five Mexican sombreros, ten Mexican blankets and at least twenty silver chains. Not that odd for souvenirs and gift giving purposes, but the exuberant purchases were done all at once, in a ten-minute time frame from the beach peddlers. I was sitting on the beach talking to two cute guys that I had met, when suddenly I looked up and there came my mother with the said wares covering her body from head to toe. Blankets around her neck, sombreros stacked high atop her head and silver chains draped over both arms. She walked towards me with arms out-stretched to the sides, so the necklaces would stay in place, displaying her purchases. At seventeen I was not impressed, but rather absolutely mortified. However, it was great for story telling purposes and laughing about her Mexican shopping spree much later.

Sometimes she would explode in angry outbursts, followed by days of slumping in a chair never to speak of the incident again. Once my dad took her to the hospital (finally) where they locked her up in the psychiatric ward. To my mother this was devastating. To us it brought hope; we thought maybe she could be fixed. They eventually sent her home with a bottle of Lithium, the mental health mood-swing pill of the day. She took a few and then threw the bottle away.

The Rolly Lake Trail Riders eventually dissolved as we were all becoming older with more responsibilities. The next rite of passage would be babysitting jobs and my first waitressing position. My father was thrilled, to say the least. "Oh, to be a waitress," my father lamented. He was so proud of me and excited that I had finally made it!

The Mandarin Palace in Mission B.C. was a highly acclaimed Chinese restaurant where underage young people could order alcoholic beverages and Chicken Chow Mein all in one fell swoop. At the end of the night the waitresses could take home all the food that had been prank ordered. My family was even more impressed by my new-found occupation as I would bring home bags of silver foil containers with Chicken Chow Mein, Sweet and Sour Pork, Almond Guy Ding, and Pork Fried Rice. Settling in to watch *Happy Days* with a heaping plate of Chinese Food, all was well!

My father would have been thrilled if I had stayed working at the Mandarin Palace as a full-time career, but I soon found out that waitressing was not an easy job, especially after I spilled a bowl of hot, sweet and sour sauce on a bald man's head. He was mildly annoyed but still gave me a fifty cent tip! I was awkward and nervous when some of the boys from my school came in to order drinks. I was too desperately shy to turn them away. It was easier to quit and go back to my leisurely life of being a teenager.

My best friend in Grade Twelve was a beautiful petite blonde by the name of Brianne. She was as pretty as her name. I on the other hand, always felt like the plain friend trailing behind with my permed dark curly hair, flat chest, and somewhat larger hips. As we walked through the dark corridors of Mission Senior Secondary High School, in platform shoes and high waisted blue jeans, my obvious insecurities only seemed to increase her beauty.

She had long blonde hair, and enormous blue eyes that were surrounded by extra-long eyelashes magnified with layers of Great Lash Mascara. Even though she too was flat chested, she could pull it off with lots of cute jewelry and very fashionable clothing. I wore two padded bras.

Every day, bringing with me my sack lunch of a tuna fish sandwich and a C-Plus orange pop, we would sit side by side at TV trays on her parent's floral couch, in front of the television to watch our favourite soap opera, *The Young and the Restless*.

After we settled in, Brianne's mother would carry out her lunch of homemade macaroni and cheese, with a pickle and tomato wedge on the side for garnish, making my oily, mayonnaise-clad tuna sandwich on dry bread very unappealing. In thirty short minutes, after Brianne sipped her last drops of tea, we would then tootle back up the hill to school to finish the last block of the day.

Back at school, we would be meshed together with the nerds, cool kids, jocks, pot heads, party girls, and artsy-fartsies that made up the graduating class. Other shy girls like myself floated throughout the halls being inconspicuous, trying to blend in and hoping no one would notice them. That didn't stop us from eyeing up all the cute boys, who only had eyes for girls like Brianne. I was never quite sure where I fit in, so I made the attempt to be nice to everyone. Endearingly being called Motor Mouth, Bubble Butt, and Edith from the hit show, *All in the Family*, referring to Edith Bunker, for some reason, I took the nick names as compliments. At the end of the day I would catch the bus back to the community of Stave Falls, to my horse and the nightly television programs with my parents.

GRADE TWELVE WAS AN EVENTFUL YEAR WITH MY BEST FRIEND. We got caught shoplifting at Seven Oaks Shopping Center, even though we were trying to put the products back (Lee Press-on Nails) as the store detective breathed down our necks a short distance behind us. We were grabbed red-handed and grilled by the security staff. Our punishment, as a way to give back to society, was a stint as volunteer Candy Stripers at the local hospital, the reasoning being that this participation in an act of service would combat our evil ways.

We were once asked on a date with two cool boys, only to have it turn into a complete debacle. Being promised a drive into Vancouver for dinner, it then became them wanting to have sex with us, and us not wanting to have sex with them. In turn, they told the whole school that we did, even though we did not. I will not deny that my short-lived bad girl persona, imposed on me by the lies those boys told, moved my shyness up a notch to that of being a mystery girl and less of a pretty girl's side kick.

Near the end of the year, before High School graduation, we signed up to be in the Miss Mission Beauty Pageant. Along with eight other contestants, all girls from our school, together we would be judged modelling three different outfits—an evening gown, a dress for afternoon tea, and a short set. At the end we would have to answer a skill testing question. My question was, "What do you think about today's fashion?"

Brianne was sponsored by the Rotary Club, while I was sponsored by the Logger Sports Association, for which my father was thrilled. As a young man in the forest industry, he had participated in Logger Sports competitions on many occasions, his claim to fame being log rolling.

There were photos, proud parents, and plenty of local newspaper articles in *The Fraser Valley Record*. An afternoon tea and fashion show with our sponsors was fun, and I wanted to keep the clothes, but they needed to go back to Stedman's Department Store.

And then finally, the Miss Mission Pageant. It turned out that three blondes were chosen, and seven brunettes were not. The winning ensemble was a queen and two princesses. Brianne was chosen as a princess, with duties of parades, social teas, and various do-good activities for one year, until the next year's Pageant and the crowning of a new royal family.

Being one of the losers, rather than be disappointed, I was elevated from my experiences and decided to attend Blanche McDonald's School of Modelling in Vancouver over the summer. This was a brief stepping stone and another boost to my self-esteem. I enrolled directly after Grade twelve graduation, driving my little Chevy Chevette to Vancouver for daily instructions on how to walk properly, apply makeup, and build a modelling portfolio. Apparently, I loved being on the runway, speaking into the microphone, and chatting in front of large audiences. It was fun, nerve-wracking, and perhaps somewhat of a scam. Nevertheless, as a beauty pageant loser and a beauty school dropout, both worked in my favour for finding my voice, getting out into the world, and making my mother and father happy. Never would I have imagined that, after always being the pretty girl's side kick, I would one day let my perm grow out, develop my own sense of style, and be up in front of audiences, speaking and motivating.

WITH GRADUATION FROM HIGH SCHOOL ACCOMPLISHED AND MY parent's encouragement to be a famous movie star or a waitress, I was not too sure what my next steps would be. The incident with my first love Todd Barnes had left me shell shocked, and getting another boyfriend anytime soon, or rather my dream of the house with the white picket fence, did not seem like a plausible option. My only solution, with my mother's encouragement, was to move to Vancouver and get a job at the local Bootlegger. My mother was so determined to have me experience a big-city amazing life, that she and my father bought me a car and essentially forced me to move to Vancouver after I had dropped out of Blanche McDonald. They paid rent for my apartment and when I was not working at Bootlegger, I was zipping around in my bright yellow 1978 Chevy Chevette, foot loose and fancy free. My only responsibility was showing up for work on time, and waiting anxiously for my 19th birthday so I could get into the Disco!

Bootlegger clothing store for blue jeans—this was hilarious to my father. Here he was at sixty-two years old, and his youngest daughter was leaving home at the age of seventeen, moving to Vancouver to work at a store called Bootlegger. Back in 1929, that fateful day leaving Saskatchewan, Vince's uncle had stopped in at the local bootlegger to pick up a few pints of moonshine to take on the road. How different it was now that all four of his children were grown. Linda, the oldest, was thirty years old, living next door in her mobile home, working for the Bank of Commerce in Mission. Doug was twenty-three, dating, and attending College. In another few years he would marry and build his own log house on the adjacent property, a log home made entirely from the trees on the land—old growth cedar. Ken, at 21, was still driving the Cat, dating, and eventually would build a home with his new wife-to-be, also next door to Vince and Frances. But Karen, the baby of the family, was going to live in Vancouver, the place where it had all started with his new bride Frances.

Eventually I would go on to work in a bank, hospitals, schools, and then have a career in fitness, plus two years at college earning a degree to work with special needs children. Throughout it all I carried with me that infamous Vince Bonner friendliness and optimism, but now and then I would wonder about the mental health issues that had plagued my mother and her sister, and their mother, my grandmother, questioning the fine line between sanity and insanity that so many people grapple with.

When we sit on the fence, if one day we fall, do we wonder where will we land? We look across the street at the man pushing his shopping cart or the lady with all her worldly possessions in one bag; homeless shelters and food banks; low income housing and people living on the streets. Everyone was once a fresh, clean baby. We all started somewhere....

Bootlegger clothing store, the best place to buy jeans

from Dec. 1986

OUR STORY

Back in 1971, everyone lived in blue jeans. And that's how Bootlegger started out, riding high on a wave of blue denim in British Columbia.

Our first stores were heavy on natural cedar, an uncluttered look, and the 'pant wall'—an unrivalled selection of jeans—which would soon become our trademark. We carried coordinating shirts, sweaters and accessories too.

Clothing was easy to find, and just as easy to put together. Best of all, we offered real value for money backed by an iron-clad guarantee.

It worked! Today there are Bootlegger stores across Canada. And, coast to coast, we still stock the largest collection of brand name jeans. Walk in now and you'll find a whole lot more. Looks from Europe (still with a casual accent). Careful colour choices that offer you limitless mix-and-match options. A real emphasis on quality at the best possible price. Genuinely friendly people ready to help you, and of course, our famous hassle-free refund policy.

New 'Miss Mission' will be selected

Twenty-three former Mission beauty queens and visiting "royalty" will be special guests Thursday evening when friends, relatives and judges gather in Mission Junior Secondary auditorium for the selection of Miss Mission 1978.

The winner, selected from the eight contestants, will represent Mission throughout British Columbia during the coming year. Participating in the PNE pageant will be one of the first events for the new Miss Mission.

Appearing in three outfits, including afternoon gowns, sports outfits and evening dresses, the contestants will be judged on appearance, public speaking and general deportment. Contestants are Denise Siam, Karen Bonner, Patrcia Fell, Rene Kelly, Sue Kendall, Lee Ann Logan, Brenda Scott and Holly Wolden.

Karen Bonner, 17, was born in North Vancouver. A 1978 graduate of Mission Secondary, she plans to become a stewardess. Her hobbies are horseback riding and swimming. She is sponsored by the Loggers Sports Association.

Lee Ann Logan, 18, born in Nanaimo, and sponsored by Legion Branch 57 is a 1978 Mission grad. Her plans include travel and employment with an airline company in Vancouver. Hobbies include her music, swimming and rug hooking.

Brenda Scott, 19, the eldest of the eight contestants was born in North Vancouver. A Mission grad she is employed as a secretary and plans to continue in the secretarial field. Her hobbies are dancing, sports and crochet. She represents the Mission Lions Club.

Sue Kendall, 18, sponsored by

Mission, is a 1978 grad and he hobby is cake decorating. Holl plans to make this her career an is also interested in first ai work. Acme Machine Shop Holly's sponsor.

Patricia Fell, 17, is still Mission Senior Seconda student. Future plans include c lege courses in graphic arts. H main interests are acting, work and soccer. CFVR is sp soring Patricia.

[See page A-5 for photos of M Mission contestants].

Rene Kelly, 18, born in Miss is sponsored by the Miss Indian Friendship Center. graduated this year and hop attend Fraser Valley Col where she plans to take sec ial courses. Rene's hobbie clude writing poetry and al door sports.

Colorful pageant is sche to start at 8 p.m. Thursday ing.

The Miss Mission nominee

Blanche MacDonald Modeling School

CHAPTER 18

In Memoriam

Gone but Not Forgotten

Joseph Michael Gervais 1885-1970

Following their insistent demands, Grandpa eventually left our family and moved in with Grandma and Auntie Violet in her trailer in Vernon. A few years later Grandpa Joe passed away after a fall he had in the hallway of Violet's home. He was found with a large contusion on his head, but no cause of death was reported on the coroner's report. My mother suspected foul play.

His funeral was held at St. David's Catholic Church in North Vancouver. It was an open casket. His wife Edith, my grandma, looked sad as she gently placed a rosary in his white powdery hands. Violet did not attend the service. My mother gave me a choice to view his dead body. So I did, but she chose not to. In his coffin, my grandpa had a smile on his face and his cheeks were rosy. He looked peaceful and calm, like a figure from Madame Tussaud's Wax Museum.

Edith Martha Stevens 1890-1975

After Grandpa died, Violet and Grandma carried on as a reclusive mother and daughter at the trailer park in Vernon. Eventually they moved from Vernon to a trailer park in White Rock, British Columbia. We would visit periodically, and Auntie Violet would tell us stories of her childhood with my mother. When we got in the car to go home, my mother would say that everything she told us during the visit—all the stories—were lies. Complete fibs.

Eventually Grandma came down with pneumonia and was hospitalised. Auntie Violet kept her death a secret from us for three weeks. She was dead and buried before we found out she had passed. There was no Will so my mother assumed that Violet got everything from both of their parents. My mom was always sad about the photographs, so we took a trip out to White Rock to see if we could get some of the many old photographs from Auntie Violet.

When we got to the trailer Auntie Violet was not there. One of her neighbours saw us knocking on the door and looking around so she came out to see who we were. When we told her that we were nieces and nephews and my mother was Violet's sister, she looked at us, horrified. Apparently, my Aunt Violet had told this neighbour that my mother had been brutally murdered, my father had died in a plane crash and all of us children had been burned to death in a fire!

We drove home in an eerie silence, unnerved. Eventually we tried to visit Auntie Vi again but by then she was just too old and did not speak at all anymore, not even to tell a lie.

Vincent Alphonse Bonner 1916-1988

My dad's nine lives sadly came to an end one year after he was diagnosed with a brain tumour. He was only 72 years old and was full of life when it ended. The tumour caused loss of his speech abilities, which saddened us because he was such an incredible storyteller. He would write notes to communicate, but it was not the same. Dad had done some bulldozing for the Gordon Hardy family from Stave Falls. The Hardy family adored my dad. The elder Mr. Hardy took it upon himself to visit dad weekly for the last year of dad's life. Being a spiritual man, he would bring his Bible, and although dad could not speak, Mr. Hardy shared stories of a loving God and an amazing afterlife. Years later, Mr. Hardy told me how happy his stories had made my dad, and how dad had nodded in agreement.

Most of us were in denial, as he wasn't supposed to die, or so we thought. Even when he was lying on his death bed in the palliative care ward at Lions Gate Hospital in North Vancouver, I thought that he would miraculously sit up in bed, tell a joke or two, and then walk out the door. He tried desperately to hang on. I whispered in his ear, near the end, that it would be okay if he left us now, that we would all be okay, that I would take care of our mom. I thanked him for being the best dad ever. After I left the room my mother went in, and twenty minutes later he passed.

My mother struggled terribly with the loss of her husband of 43 years. She became very ill with her mental health and ran up and down the street yelling at people, complete strangers, telling them that everyone took advantage of her husband's kindness and THEY were the reason for his demise. Our family was traumatised emotionally from his death and our mother's way of coping.

His memorial service was so well attended that not everyone could fit into the room. We played all of his favourite songs and we had an open mike. I still wish to this day that I had stood up to say something. But in my heart I know that he knew how much he was loved and adored.

Violet Ann Gervais 1915-2000

We heard that Auntie Violet had been moved to a geriatric hospital in White Rock. We did go to visit her once just before she died, and we were treated poorly because no one ever visited Violet, therefore the nurses and staff thought that we were a mean and neglectful family. They would not have known her past and I am glad that they were nice to her.

I often wondered why my mother and her sister were not close, and all I ever really knew was that my aunt was notorious for telling lies, and she and my mother never bonded like sisters quite often do. My mother spoke very little about her sister. If I could, I would love to ask my mother now about the details of their relationship and why it never really took off.

Violet had a Will, leaving everything to the SPCA, the society for the prevention of cruelty to animals. Well, almost everything. She had always promised to leave my brother Ken her Cadillac, so she did. My mother received a letter stating that something was to come in the mail for her from Violet's estate. Eventually a big parcel was delivered and inside was an ancient dilapidated wheelchair. How odd and seemingly gruesome. Violet's last Will and Testament was the making for an old movie with Lana Turner and Bette Davis!

Mary Frances Lillian Bonner 1922-2009

My mother lived on and survived twenty-two years after my father passed away. Our family shifted a lot after my dad died. He was the glue that held us all together and when the glue was no longer adhesive, everything just kind of fell apart. My brothers and I were married or dating and we had children of our own. Our sister Linda was living in northern British Columbia so the four of us were distracted, living, doing, and being. But soon our mother became her own person and our family naturally began to fall into place again.

There was a transformation and an anger within our mom. She still struggled with her moods, highs and lows. Her anger and her annoyance at the world was almost unbearable at times. And then, instead of highs and lows, she only became high. She was on a perpetual up-swing. Laughing too much, spending too much, happy and loving everything and everyone. She hardly ever slept, stating that she could sleep when she was dead. It was as if a switch had been turned on and she became the light, or the fire cracker that would never stop popping. We took this with a grain of salt. She was comical and exhausting to be around. Her sense of humour was contagious and all three of my children received a little bit of their grandmother's kookiness and share many funny grandma stories that they hold dear in their hearts. I asked my mother once if she ever prayed, and she said that whenever she attended MRCC, the church that I attended, (which she did periodically), she would pray the sinner's prayer, because it was better to be safe than sorry.

Often I had lived with her and she had lived with me. In the end, she had a stroke. She lasted about two weeks after the stroke and we were all a little surprised when she died peacefully one night in her hospital bed. Before the stroke she lived the last two years of her life hardly being able to see or hear and she complained of not having any taste buds. She was failing long before the stroke.

Somebody posted on Facebook recently that it was the anniversary of their mother's death; how sad that date in time had become, how hard, how melancholy, and how the date would always be remembered. The likes, comments, and replies were heartfelt with remorse and memories of the beautiful, caring mother she once was. Thoughts were expressed of heaven and a sublime afterlife, of sunshine and rainbows. Surely she is there with the angels in all their glory? The fate of the dear, sweet departed mother was written in the clouds because of her amazing goodness. So too for our dear mother.

The date of my mother's death I cannot remember. The month yes, it was July. The rest is a foggy blur, her tired, ageing, failing body, a sad and distant memory. Her life, what I can remember of it, was a box of treasured gifts, to be opened here and there at my leisure; the image of her in a bright yellow dress (my father's favourite colour) sitting next to my dad sipping a drink out of a coconut; her loose house dress as she leaned and stretched over the railing of our back porch, hanging up the wash, the white sheets and towels flapping in the wind on a brisk October morning; my mother, sitting at the beach with a stack of newspapers, French Fries sprinkled with vinegar, hair blowing, no sun screen, no sunglasses and no beach umbrella , just an old worn towel, sand, rocks and a lifeguard nearby, perched on his post with a megaphone in hand and a whistle ready to be blown.

We had a wonderful memorial for her. The pastor, my siblings, and some of my friends said many nice things about her and shared some of her more comical idiosyncrasies. We all had personal memories and good feelings about Fran Bonner. My children fondly remember her saying to the ambulance drivers as they came to take her away, "Oh darn, if I had known you were coming I would have dressed up a bit."

I leave you with my mother's mottos:

"Laugh too much, spend your money, love everyone and everything, don't worry about not getting enough sleep, you can sleep when you are dead. Why fight about religion when we are all just trying to get to the same place. If you know that they are coming, then dress up a bit."

Life Lessons from my Father:

The things I learned from my father were not filled with deep, philosophical meaning. They were more to do with his character and perspective on life. He taught by example how to treat others, display affection, work hard, and how to have fun and stay hopeful at all costs. His way of coping was with a never-give-up attitude, and he had an incredible ability to find humour in most situations.

He gave me permission to cry my heart out, grieve life's disappointment, and move past my losses. He taught me that everything changes, and yet some things stay the same.

My own thoughts about success should travel between my heart and my mind; they are not about monetary gain or what is in my pocket book, but rather about relationships, experiences, and the community in which I dwell. Love is mostly the answer.

The story I choose to tell is valuable, it belongs to me, so I can passionately tell it with every ounce of conviction that I can muster.

Fighting the pirate for the damsel in distress

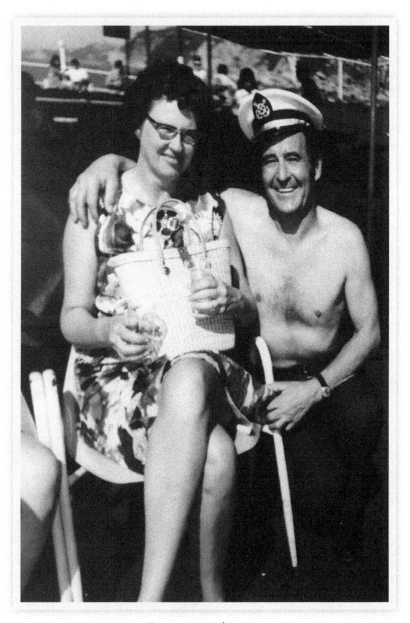

The good guy always wins

REFERENCES/BIBLIOGRAPHY

Looking for Normal

Chapter 1
#1. Borderline Personality Disorder, BPD OVERVIEW—Borderline
     Personality; https://www.borderlinepersonalitydisorder.com
#2. Coca-Cola; www.coca-colacompany.com ;
     https://www.worldofcoca-cola.com

Chapter 2
#3. Great Depression — Facts and Summaries; www.history.com ;
     www.canadianencyclopedia.com
#4. Abandoned Child Syndrome; https://en.wikipedia.org.
#5. Province's name chosen by Queen Victoria https://www.quora.com ;
#6. Sen-Sen Pop Culture https://en.m.wikipedia.org
#7. A Brief History of Alcohol and Alcoholic Beverages—Alcohol: A Short
     History; Drug-Free World www.drugfreeworld.org

Chapter 3
#8. Vancouver is the Third rainiest city in Canada: Google
#9. This Week in History 1919 Shaughnessy Heights; www.vancouversun.com
     metro story
#10. British Columbia Electric Railway; https://en.m.wikipedia.org
#11. How Seasonal Disorder Affects Bipolar Disorder, Everyday Health;
     https://www.everydayhealth.com

Chapter 4
#12. The Trail of 1858 British Columbia's Gold Rush Past by Mark Forsythe &
     Greg Dickson. Harbour Publishing. 2007
#13. Historical Atlas of the North American Railroad by Derek Hayes. Douglas
     & McIntyre Publishers Inc. Vancouver/Toronto. 2010
#14. The Great Years from 1933 to 1943 Gold Mining in the Bridge River
     Valley by Lewis Green. Indigo. 2001

#15. Historical Atlas of British Columbia and the Pacific Northwest by Derek Hayes. Douglas & McIntyre Publishers Inc. Cavendish Books. Vancouver 2003

Chapter 5
#16. Actress, Frances Farmer IMDB, September 19, 1913—August 1, 1970.
#17. Boeing Canada—History; www.boeing.ca
#18. The War Worker Poem, author Unknown, circa 1940; https://canadianpoems.ca
#19. Prohibition; https://www.meriam-webster.com; https://dictionary.cambridge.org; https://oxforddictionaries.com (speakeasies)

Chapter 6
#20. A History of Logging on the Westcoast, working in the Woods by Ken Druska. Harbour Publishing. 1992. Published with the assistance of the Canada Council and the Government of British Columbia.
#21. The Backyard Lumberjack, the Ultimate Guide to Felling, Bucking, Splitting, and Stacking by Frank Philbrick and Stephen Philbrick. Storey Publishing, 2006.

Chapter 9
#22. The History of Lost Lagoon, Stanley Park's Water Jewel—Scout Magazine; www.scoutmagazine.ca; stanleyparkecology.ca; www.vancouverisawesome.com.
#23. Lost Lagoon poem by Emily Pauline Johnson. Poem Hunter; https://www.poemhunter.com
#24. Malkin Bowl; https://www.malkinbowl.com.
#25. Moodyville—Heritage Vancouver; www.heritagevancouver.org.
26. Addiction and Mood Disorders, a Guide for Clients and Families by Dennis C. Daley with Antoine Douaihy. Oxford University Press, 2006.
#27. Hidden Lives: Coming Out on Mental Illness. Edited by Lenore Rowntree and Andrew Boden; forward by Gabor Maté. Brindle and Glass Publishing Co. 2012.
#28. Social Work in the 21st Century: An Introduction to Social Welfare, Social Issues and the Profession by Morley D. Glicken. Sage Publications, 2007.

Chapter 10
#29. Dance with a Dolly by Tony Pastor. From the movie *Her Lucky Night*, 1945. Performed by The Andrews Sisters.
#30. Second Narrows Bridge Collapse—The Canadian Encyclopedia; www.thecanadianencyclopedia.ca.
#31. Tears of a Clown by Smokey Robinson and the Miracles. 1965.

Chapter 11
#32. The 1960s: Facts and Summaries. www.history.com.

Chapter 13
#33. Do Cats Really Have Nine Lives? https://wonderopolis.org.
#34. Lynn Canyon Suspension Bridge and Lynn Canyon Park; https://en.mwikipedia.org; www.lynncanyon.ca.
#35. History—North Vancouver, Museum and Archives nvma.ca; www.greatervancouverparks.com.

Chapter 14
#36. Doctor Benjamin Spock: Child Care and Controversy. Dr. Spock Biography; www.legacy.com. https://britannica.com.
#37. Mad Magazine, The History of Mad; https://www.en.m.wikipedia.
#38. Rowan and Martin's, Laugh-In IMDB.
#39. The Original Beauty Queen: The Story of Elizabeth Arden; hanna-online.org; Elizabeth Arden—Wikipedia; https://www.wikipedia.org; www.fashionmodeldirectory.com.

Chapter 15
#40. Barbie Doll—Wikipedia; https://en.m.wikipedia.org; https://barbie.mattel.com.
#41. Boeing 747 Jumbo Jet History; www.modernairliners.com. Boeing 747—Wikipedia; https://en.wikipedia.org/wiki-Boeing_747

Chapter 16
#42. Hope Slide – Wikipedia; https://en.wikipedia.org/wiki/Hope_Slide. Case Study 1965 Hope Slide British Columbia; https://opentextbc.ca.

CPSIA information can be obtained
at www.ICGtesting.com
Printed in the USA
LVHW03s0216200818
587123LV00003B/4/P